Tomorrow Will Be Too Late

Tomorrow
Will Be Too Late

EAST MEETS WEST ON GLOBAL ECOLOGY

Rolf Edberg   *Alexei Yablokov*

Translated by Sergei Chulaki

THE UNIVERSITY OF ARIZONA PRESS   TUCSON

Copyright © 1988 by Progress Publishers, Moscow, USSR

Published by agreement with Progress Publishers

∞ This book is printed on acid-free, archival-quality paper.

Manufactured in the U.S.A.

Library of Congress Cataloging-in-Publication Data

Edberg, Rolf, 1912–

    Tomorrow will be too late : East meets West on global ecology /
Rolf Edberg, Alexei Yablokov : translated by Sergei Chulaki.

      p.   cm.

    Translated from the Russian.

    Includes index.

    ISBN 0-8165-1217-5.—ISBN 0-8165-1228-0 (pbk.)

    1. Man—Influence on nature. 2. Human ecology—Moral and ethical
aspects. 3. Ecology—Moral and ethical aspects. 4. Environmental
policy. 5. Pollution—Moral and ethical aspects. I. ÍAblokov, A.
V. (Alekseĭ Vladimirovich) II. Title. III. Title: Global ecology.

GF80.E3 1991

363.7—dc20   90-44528

                                                CIP

CONTENTS

About the Authors

ROLF EDBERG has served Sweden as a member of Parliament, ambassador to Norway, president of the Stockholm International Peace Institute, delegate to the United Nations, president of the Swedish Press Club, and chairman of the Environmental Committee of the Royal Swedish Academy of Sciences, among other positions. He has won numerous awards, including the Dag Hammarskjold Medal in 1978. He is the author of six books, including *Spillran av ett moln,* published in English under the title *On the Shred of a Cloud*, the book that helped stir the Swedes to press for what eventually became the United Nations World Conference on the Human Environment. Mr. Edberg lives in Karlstad, Sweden.

ALEXEI YABLOKOV has taken part in zoological expeditions to Central Asia, the Far East, India, and Sri Lanka, among other places. His interest in the ecological problems of the world has led to cooperation with other scientists from the United States, Sweden, and Poland in protecting mammals. He has written several monographs on the theory of evolution, the biology of dolphins, and the problems of ecology. He has been a corresponding member of the Academy of Sciences of the USSR since 1984 and now heads the continuous ontogenesis laboratory at the Koltsov Institute of Biology, the USSR Academy of Sciences. He has been deputy chairman of the committee of the Supreme Soviet on ecology and rational utilization of natural resources since 1989. He lives in Moscow.

PREFACE TO THE ENGLISH TRANSLATION

A very short time has passed, indeed, since Rolf and I exchanged our last words in this dialogue and since this book was published in 1988, simultaneously in Sweden and the USSR. How much has changed in the world! History once again has shown us that the society in which we live cannot remain unchanged. The absence of change leads to a situation where changes, when they do come, are very great.

With the fall of the Berlin Wall and the breakthrough of glasnost the world was appalled by that ecological abyss that we in the East have dug out for ourselves as we attempted to secure the triumph of the Socialist idea at the cost of millions of destroyed human lives and environmentally insensitive economic development. However, the threat to the environment comes as well from the most developed industrial technologies, and additionally from the expanding poverty in third- and fourth-world countries. At present an explosion of understanding is taking place in front of our very eyes, understanding that it is impossible for the world to go on as it has. It is impossible because, as a result of our activity, the ozone layer is becoming thinner, the climate is changing, species are disappearing, biological nature is being degraded, and toxic waste is spreading over the whole planet—the forests, rivers, and oceans are dying and deserts are spreading.

Never before have we observed such scientific, social, and political activity in defense of the nature on our planet as in the past two years. Not a month has passed without there being in one country or another international conferences arranged to discuss these problems. An understanding of the importance of these problems of the environment to people and governments is quickly spreading through all levels of society—from the masses of ordinary people to political leaders.

All of this offers hope that just as opposition between eastern and western Europe is collapsing before our eyes so, too, could the world quickly shift from the arms race to a race to the defense of Nature, our common habitat. And countries in the very near future will compete among themselves, not in the number of tanks or missiles, but in how quickly they can transform scientific knowledge into practical recommendations, and these recommendations into practical policies.

For me, the words I have just spoken are not just words. The perestroika begun by Mikhail Gorbachev brought us to the point in 1989 where I, along with Andrei Sakharov, Valentin Rasputin, Yevgeny Yevtushenko, and a whole group of other intellectuals were elected to the Soviet Parliament. An opportunity has arisen to make Soviet politics, both internally and externally, "greener" (more environmentally aware). And in the coming years I have decided to devote myself to this cause. Even if I do not succeed in doing everything that I have planned, I will not have to reproach myself for not having tried.

In May 1990 in Washington, 150 parliamentary members from forty-two countries signed the Declaration of Ecological Interdependence. In many countries around the world preparations are being made for a worldwide United Nations Conference on the Environment that will meet in 1992 in Brazil. Among the documents being prepared for this conference is the *Code of Ecological Ethics*. This is a real step to the new morality about which we spoke in our book. The Brazilian conference could become the turning point in global development from ideological confrontation and the arms race between East and West and from economic confrontation between North and South, to a race for worldwide security. As we are now beginning to understand it, there can be no military, economic, or social security without ecological security.

Much has been irretrievably destroyed and lost in nature, and this threatens the future existence of humankind. We must be more decisive, forceful, and imaginative in seeking unconventional solutions to these problems, and we must act quickly.

In conclusion, I would like to express deep appreciation to Barbara

Beatty and Douglas Weiner for their assistance in the preparation of this edition of the book.

ALEXEI YABLOKOV

Moscow, USSR

June 1990

As Alexei has pointed out, a radical remolding has occurred in great parts of Europe since he and I finished our dialogue in early 1988. Things that for us at that time were wishes and visions have suddenly become realities.

In the course of our talks, I asked whether it would not be reasonable that the countries of Eastern Europe take part in some way in the cooperation that is now taking shape in Western Europe, and I spoke out for the freedom of all individuals to pass unrestricted from one room to another in our common European home. None of us could imagine that these goals would be achieved only a little more than one year later. The threat of nuclear war, which then threw a dark shadow over the human existence, seems today to be a past nightmare.

On the other hand, and at the same time, the environmental problems have reached new dimensions. When the wall that divided Europe was broken up, the frightening state of things was brought into the open, which up to that time had been hidden by those in power. Parts of the continent are ecologically so deteriorated and unhealthy that they ought to be evacuated. We can surely expect a new kind of refugee: the environmental refugee. Since the problem of a few of the thirty-odd countries is the problem of all, Europeans should regard the solution as a common task.

My friend Alexei has, since we concluded our dialogue, been given a formidable task as vice-chairman of the environmental committee of the people's congress in the largest country of the world with its enormous problems. It would have to be a man of his great knowledge, devotion, and will to meet such a challenge with a firm conviction that the problems should and can be solved.

During the last years it has become more and more obvious that we are coming to a fork in the road and the choice we make can determine the future of civilization.

The final responsibility for the destiny of our planet rests with the policymakers. Only they have the power to decide whether the state of the world will improve or decline.

To be sure, what has happened and is happening in our environment will be recognized at long last as many governments try to find at least partial solutions to a few of the problems. California, for instance, gives proof of an administration that is seriously and forcefully tackling the problems. There are signs of hope but still too few.

Decision makers on all levels, especially on the national level and in the great industrialized countries, must be kept under constant pressure from alert and alarmed scientists of insight and knowledge. I single out scientists because they have a special responsibility as the pathfinders we send to find a path into the future. But the common view of all people is important because it has a tremendous power when united against conditions that are considered unbearable—that's a lesson we have recently learned in Europe.

Pressure groups and lobbyists have mounted a campaign that takes advantage of the scientific uncertainty that always accompanies observations and conclusions that are not, and for obvious reasons cannot be, supported by experiments. Because there are rulers who are a little too willing to buy such arguments, this campaign is obviously gathering strength. A strong offensive by environmentalists in the scientific community, as well as at the grass-roots level, is all the more necessary to counter this movement.

At the core of common opinion are the young people. It is their world it is all about. We saw students as the vanguards in the peaceful revolutions in Hungary and Czechoslovakia; we followed their unarmed fight in the Square of the Heavenly Peace in Beijing, where a petrified ruling junta could only answer with tanks and machine guns. In the capitalist world many young people are in search of alternative values and lifestyles, rejecting long-established patterns.

The younger generation is not burdened with the guilt of my own generation. The Russian poet Yevgeny Yevtushenko has called them "the immaculate generation," while a French paper after a student revolt in Paris against racism spoke about "the moral generation." Across the frontiers young people meet, expressing their opposition to commercialism in the West and bureaucracy in the East. They represent the hope for the survival of the planet Earth.

But the time left to us is limited and shrinking. To put it in the words of Lester Brown of the World Watch Institute: "We do not have generations; we only have years in which to attempt to turn things around."

ROLF EDBERG
Stockholm, Sweden
May 1990

PREFACE TO THE RUSSIAN EDITION

In 1987 Progress Publishers in Moscow proposed that we tape-record a dialogue and write a book based on that dialogue about the problems facing mankind as we approach the third millennium. Norstedts Publishers in Stockholm supported this idea and published the book in Sweden at the same time it appeared in the Soviet Union.

Each of us, East and West, had spent much time studying the problems of the interaction between man and nature until finally both understood that ecological health could not be achieved in just one country, whatever its size or its distance from other countries.

We—a Swede and a Russian—represent different ideologies, have different backgrounds and different life experiences. The Russian is a scientist who specializes in ecological studies. The Swede is the author of many books on questions of survival, although his main field is domestic and international politics. We thought it natural that this combination of factors would lead to different approaches to the same problems, and we were prepared to discuss the issues that divided us.

At first the task seemed too formidable. We had never met before and knew nothing about one another. On the other hand, it was a challenge to try and find out if two men who did not hold any official posts and represented only themselves could come to a consensus on questions that concerned millions of people in the modern world. Like two traveling companions on our little planet, we would ask each other questions that concerned many people in both East and West: what is the future of our planet after we enter the new millennium?

This book is the product of many hours of discussion in Moscow and

Stockholm. Our meetings were sponsored by the Union of Soviet Writers, which invited Rolf to the USSR, and by the Royal Swedish Academy of Sciences, which invited Alexei to Sweden.

One day in the autumn of 1987 we sat down in front of the microphone with a list of tentative questions in front of us. Later, we were astounded by the almost total agreement of our views. The exchange broadened our horizons and we hope that readers will benefit from the ideas that we came up with.

We wish to express our gratitude to interpreters L. Zhdanov (Moscow), who first introduced us to each other, to M. Salin and M. Dixelius (Stockholm), who made our dialogue possible and thus contributed to getting this book written.

We also thank here the persons to whom we owe a debt of gratitude—O. Katagoshchin and E. Nikulin, A. Edberg, A. Poulsson, M. Olsson, and C. Edelstam, and also to the late E. D. Bakulina (Yablokova)—for their cooperation.

ROLF EDBERG
ALEXEI YABLOKOV
Stockholm
February 28, 1988

DAY

1

OUR GENERATION LIVES ACCORDING
TO A NEW CHRONOLOGY, STARTING FROM THE YEAR
OF HIROSHIMA RATHER THAN THE BIRTH
OF CHRIST OR MOHAMMED.

—ROLF EDBERG

THE TIME HAS COME TO LOOK FOR POINTS IN
COMMON BETWEEN EAST AND WEST IN AREAS
WHERE THEY DIFFER THE MOST. AND THIS MUST BE
DONE NOT ONLY BY POLITICIANS ... BUT BY
ALL PEOPLE—SCIENTISTS, JOURNALISTS, WRITERS.

—ALEXEI YABLOKOV

■

A Y   In 1986, I chanced upon your book, *Brev till Columbus* (Letters to Columbus), which captured my imagination. I wanted to discuss it with the author, because it contained many things that I accepted without reservation, and many others to which I took exception. At any rate, the book did not leave me indifferent because it showed that my professional interest in the environment came much closer to the other problems of mankind than I had thought.

Of course, your book was not the only factor that led me to think that way. The past several years have seen some developments that have prompted every intelligent person to make up his mind about where he should stand in this onrush of ideas.

In 1987 a world peace forum was held in Moscow. I realized then that the thoughts in my mind also occupied the minds of other people concerned about the future of the world, of the environment. And I thought that the sooner we exchanged views, possibly in a heated debate, with plenty of give-and-take, the sooner we would understand each other and thus help preserve peace and life on Earth. This is why I immediately responded positively to the proposal of Progress Publishers [Moscow] to write, jointly with you, a very frank, possibly controversial book about man and nature. And that's how it all started.

R E   I was very glad when I came to the peace forum that winter and met you, Alexei. After our discussion one evening we decided to meet again.

The forum itself whose keynote was "for a nuclear free world, for the survival of humankind" was a very interesting undertaking, with almost a thousand participants from about eighty countries representing different ideologies. Scientists, writers, artists, doctors, industrialists, and prominent representatives of the clergy exchanged their views in frank round-table discussions. There was no attempt on the part of the sponsors to direct the course of the debate, much less to stifle criticism. I was particularly impressed by statements made by Andrei Sakharov, Chinghiz Aitmatov, Norman Mailer, Graham Greene, Dieter Lattmann, and Günter Grass.

I was one of a group that had been invited to Moscow by the Union of Soviet Writers. Among those who signed the invitation was the poet Andrei Voznesenski. His speech at the forum made a profound impression upon me. He finished his speech with a poem in which he very skillfully played up the figure 1987, which symbolized, as it were, a count-down for humankind: 10, 9, 8, 7 . . . Could we stop before reaching zero?

I am positive that many people of our time, who are not just on the threshold of another century, but on the threshold of a new millennium, are asking themselves: what will become of our planet when we cross into the third millennium? For the question at issue is the survival of man as a living species. There are no specialists on this question. This is a question that concerns the whole human race. It concerns all of us together and each one of us separately.

And we, too, Alexei, are taking up these questions as two of the five billion concerned citizens of the planet Earth. We represent different systems, and we have different life experiences, and this is why we may not necessarily have fully identical views on everything. However, upon our first meeting, when we were just sizing up one another, it became clear that neither of us wished to engage in fruitless polemics between so-called "East" and so-called "West." Others do that, and do that with blinders on their eyes. As for us, in our short dialogue we shall concentrate on things common to all people.

This is why it would be natural if we started out with concrete facts and spoke about things that threaten our planet and all living things on it, if we told about how each of us interprets the nature of these threats, so we could explain further how each of us understands what should be done to ward them off.

A Y The most widely discussed threat is that of a nuclear holocaust. And I believe that this threat can be warded off.

R E I fully share your view. In our century in which two world wars have been fought, the threat of a third war, which, of course, would be a nuclear war, is so formidable that it comes up for discussion first. After all, if humankind does not eliminate the nuclear threat, all the other efforts to improve the world we live in will be futile.

We must recall here that we have had more than our share of armed conflicts. However limited they may be, they might easily spread. Ironically, in the year 1986, which the United Nations proclaimed an International Year of Peace, there were thirty-six wars and armed conflicts, with five million men from forty-one countries taking part. Moreover, many other countries sent weapons to the theaters of military operations. Hundreds of thousands of young men thus joined the shadows of those who had for centuries been doomed to senseless death by violence, while the great powers continued to develop new, ever more destructive weapons.

And all this pales before the main threat, the threat of nuclear war. Nuclear weapons cannot in any way be compared with any other weapons that existed in the past. Nuclear war is different from any other war ever fought, not only in the scope of destruction, but in its very substance. For the first time in history, one of the species living on this planet has developed an instrument for its total self-destruction.

I think we have every right to say that our generation lives according to a new chronology, starting from the Year of Hiroshima, and not from the birth of Christ or Mohammed.

A Y Yes, Hiroshima is the starting point of modern civilization. But there is another such starting point. This is Albert Einstein with his warning that there might be an atomic war. Also Antoine-Henri

Becquerel who discovered radioactivity. And Vernadski who, with his vision of the future, was the first to realize that the radioactivity liberated by man might spell the end of the world.

When I think that nuclear war is possible, the very idea of it raises questions to which I find no answers. In 1984, it seemed clear that nuclear war would be suicidal because it would inevitably be followed by a "nuclear winter." However, for some reason the nuclear arms race is still on. Starting with the 1960s military strategists in the United States and the Soviet Union were aware that nuclear war would be the last war on Earth. They knew that and nevertheless continued to prepare for it. And this is what I cannot understand!

Nor can I understand—either as a human being or as a scientist—why our countries need thousands of nuclear warheads when it is well known that if a country launched nuclear missiles it would perish even if its antagonist failed to retaliate.

If a person understands that he cannot put up a house at a certain spot because it will inevitably fall to pieces, he will build it at another spot. And if a scientist sees that the method he used to solve a problem is ineffective he will look for another method, another way. If a designer understands that a perpetual motion machine cannot be built, he abandons the idea. Absurdly, our strategists understand that nuclear weapons cannot be used, and yet they produce them, store them up, and test them. All this is beyond me.

RE The scientists, many of whom emigrated from Nazi-ridden Europe, created the atomic bomb in the United States. They did that because they feared that Hitler might have such a weapon, and that would mean the end of the world. The same scientists were the first to demand that the atomic bomb not ever be used. The very *idea* of its existence was to have an intimidating effect. The bombing of Hiroshima was a war crime and political blunder: Japan had already been crushed.

Scientists such as Einstein, Szilard, and Bohr prophesied, after Hiroshima, that a nuclear arms race would smother the world, and called for placing the new type of energy under international control. Einstein said that the explosion of the atomic bomb over Hiroshima might eliminate all the obsolete political ideas. There was still time to change one's mind. In January of Year One after Hiroshima, the United Nations General Assembly met in its first session. Significantly, its first unanimous vote was cast in favor of the idea of setting up a commission that was to draft a treaty banning atomic weapons. Six months later, a new bomb was blasted on one of the atolls of the Marshall Islands. That bomb destroyed not only the atoll but also the UN Atomic Energy Commission.

Thus a nuclear arms race began. Have you ever considered the fact that the testing of atomic bombs in the so-called peace time released two hundred times as much explosive energy as that in the five years of the Second World War? Only one monstrous bomb of fifty-eight megatons dropped over Novaya Zemlia sixteen years after Hiroshima was equal to 3,000 bombs of the type that destroyed this city, and twenty times as great as the total explosive energy of all the bombs dropped in the course of the Second World War. Very possibly that explosion precipitated more radioactive fallout in Scandinavia than did Chernobyl. The winds scattered strontium 90 and cesium 137 throughout the world. They penetrated the tissue of all living organisms and were passed through mother's milk to new citizens of our planet.

When the Conference on Disarmament opened in Geneva in 1961, eight nonaligned nations urged the participants to come to terms over ending all nuclear weapons tests and to work out a memorandum on controls concerning the observance of this agreement. And since Sweden was the initiator of this memorandum, I had a chance to talk with the heads of the delegations of the two superpowers. However, the Russians, very politely, and the Americans less so, gave us to understand that what they were doing was none of our business and that we had better stay out of what seemed to be their private affair.

But gradually, the great powers found out that testing in the atmosphere threatened their own safety and agreed to stop it. As for underground nuclear testing, it continues to this day. Even in 1986, International Year of Peace, nuclear powers exploded twenty-three nuclear devices, which, however, was the lowest figure since 1961.

A Y Was it because the USSR had imposed a moratorium on nuclear testing?

R E Exactly! But the other side did not follow the Soviet example, so that eventually the Soviet Union had to resume testing. Meanwhile, the French continued their outrageous nuclear blasts on the Polynesian island of Mururua.

So as you see, everything goes on the same old way. Sometimes the tests are defended with the claim that the underground testing carried out by the opposite side cannot allegedly be verified. This is absolute nonsense.

In my native Vïrmland stands a red house with white shutters on its windows. It stands in the midst of a forest as far away from sources of noise as possible. And right there inside this house are sophisticated seismic instruments that can register explosions at a distance of up to 10,000 kilometers.

Similar instruments are used in other places of the world, too. I think nonaligned countries are able to verify the observance of the ban on nuclear blasts. Technically, this is no problem at all.

A Y And yet such blasts are continuing to this day!

R E Yes, it's true. The blasts are continuing and are thus creating new political problems. In my view, priority must be given to the cessation of testing of new types of weapons if we are to be serious about disarmament.

There are too many nuclear weapons in the world already. Its stockpiles, in terms of ordinary conventional explosives, equal fifteen tons of TNT for every man, woman, or child in the world. All of us—whites, blacks, yellows, and reds, old people like myself and newborn babies—are sitting, each one of us, on an explosive charge equivalent to fifteen giant bombs of the type used in the Second World War. These fifteen bombs are sufficient to blow up a small town. The present stockpiles of nuclear weapons are sufficient to kill every citizen of our planet many times over.

AY As it happens, the situation depends not just on the will or intention of a certain government, but on the need to change the way of thinking of all mankind. Our ability to make sophisticated objects has far outstripped our spiritual maturity. One philosopher of the last century said that as technology progresses, morals degenerate. If this is so, then in our society we must pay more attention to morals and ethics than to the development of technology. We must bring our morals in alignment with our technological know-how. Jumping ahead, I must say that whatever is anti-ecological must be viewed as immoral.

If we take a look back in history we shall see that after each major discovery in the sphere of armaments people said: "Now war has lost all meaning." This is what H. Schrapnell said after he had thought of filling an artillery projectile with small pieces of metal to be scattered in flight by detonation. Frederick Engels said the same thing when an automatic rifle was invented that could shoot more than ten rounds a minute. He thought that war would become senseless. The inventors of chemical weapons also held that this potent weapon would rule out the very possibility of war. And each time they were wrong. People invented new and ever more powerful weapons and have finally arrived at the absolute nuclear weapon that we have spoken about. Now this absolute weapon has become senseless, too.

RE You are quite right: the nuclear weapon has rendered war utterly senseless. One may say that this is the result of the progress of military technology as you mentioned earlier on. The result is bleak: a weapon that can put an end to all history, to all future on this tiny speck of life in the universe. This is what makes this weapon so different from all the others.

Once I stood in Hiroshima in front of a stone with an image of a human being on it. That was a terrible sight. . . . The silhouette of a man who had been incinerated within a fraction of a second in a city whose central part was scorched at a temperature equal to that on the surface of the sun and was blown out of its foundations to as high as ten kilometers in order to drop dead in the form of ashes, debris, and radioactive fallout.

Standing in front of this shadow [of a man] I asked myself: could nuclear war turn the whole of our planet into a global Hiroshima?

Now we know that things would be even worse than that.

Academies of science representing many different countries have set up the Scientific Committee on Preservation of the Environment which has commissioned three hundred scientists from thirty countries to study the possible affects of a nuclear war on our planet. They found out that the number of immediate casualties would be far more than two billion people who might burn up in nuclear flames, be atomized or killed in fire and radioactive fallout, or who might die for lack of organized medical assistance. The smoke and ashes from burning cities, forests, fields, oil tanks, and coal dumps would then form a solid blanket over the surface of the Earth, so that only a fraction of solar light would reach the surface of the planet. Thus night would set in amidst broad daylight, and the temperatures in the northern hemisphere would drop by 20° to 40°C. A nuclear winter would set in to last for months.

Further studies made some adjustments, for the heat coming from the oceans and the winds might moderate the drop in the temperature by half, that is, down to between 10 and 20°C. What would that change anyway? The cold winter night would still be there. In the West the climatologists calculated that during the past ice age the temperatures had dropped by an average of 10°C.

AY   No, less than 10°! The average temperature in the world then dropped by a mere 2° or 3°C.

RE   So the outlook is bleak. As a biologist, you, Alexei, must know what a nuclear winter would mean for life on Earth: for the photosynthesis of land-bound plants, for the phytoplankton in the ocean, for the entire plant world that produces oxygen for our lungs and transforms salts and juices of the Earth into food for our bodies.

A Y If that happens, all life of the highest order will perish. In a few months the Earth would lose all its highest organisms. The Earth would be set back three to four billion years in its development. What would remain then would be microorganisms, so that everything would start from scratch. In addition to that we would have to take account not only of the ashes and the rain. The ozone screen would then also be destroyed, and the hard ultraviolet radiation would kill everything living on earth. This scenario does not suit us at all.

R E In other words the "nuclear winter" would turn the Earth into a kind of Flying Dutchman of outer space, a ship without a crew.

A Y The question poses itself: what is it all for? Why do we need the nuclear threat? Some say: "to protect communist ideology," others "to protect the western lifestyle." Both contentions are senseless. What we need is a new kind of political thinking. The time has come to look for points in common between East and West in areas where they differ the most. And that must be done not only, or rather not so much by politicians as by all people—scientists, journalists, writers.

R E Yes, the problem may stand out in greater relief and the madness will be even more apparent if the arms drive is contrasted to the poverty that dominates the world. Every two seconds half a billion Swedish kronas are spent on armament, and in the same two seconds a child dies in poor countries. That child could be saved if money were available. The world spends eighty times as much money on teaching children how to shoot as it does on teaching them how to read. A mere 5 percent of the money expended on armament would suffice to remove the most grievous effects of world want. What all countries spend on armament during five weeks would be quite sufficient to provide every family in the world with sufficient drinking water from hydrants or kitchen taps. Alexei, you speak about morality. Don't these figures speak about the abysmal amorality manifested in what is given preference?

A Y   And would there be enough water for all these hydrants and fau-
cets?

R E   I am sure there would be if the economy was managed the way it
should be. But we shall discuss this later.

The American social scientist Ruth Seward compared military
and social expenditures to show up our absurd approach to what we
regard as the most important things. She found out that fifteen
million people die every year who could have lived.

I cannot help recalling one clever broadside that Seward directed
at the great powers. Several years ago, in one of her studies, she
published a map of the city she called Moskington. On this map
the Moskva River and the Potomac flow into one waterway, and on
its banks you can see the Kremlin, the White House, and other
important buildings of Moscow and Washington. By joining the
capitals of the two superpowers the researcher sought to show the
absurdity of nuclear thinking. In the event of world conflagration,
both capitals would be destroyed.

The terrible thing is that the development of new types of weapons is being fanned by a small group of anonymous moguls—weapons designers, manufacturers, and the top brass—who for years
work behind closed doors in order to present the politicians with a
fait accompli. Every new type of weapon takes from ten to fifteen
years to produce.

In the West, where politicians often replace one another after a
short stay in power, it may prove more difficult to check the deployment of a newly manufactured weapon. In such countries as China
and the Soviet Union, their leaders usually hold their top jobs
longer. But even there the pressure of the top brass and arms designers is fairly strong.

A Y   I think that there is no difference between East and West in this
respect. I want to recall here that the Soviet Union began its history
with a remarkable peace initiative. In practically the first days of
Soviet government, Lenin signed the Decree on Peace whereby So-

viet Russia proposed that all the belligerent states in Europe stop their hostilities immediately.

Later, slowly, step by step, as we had to defend ourselves against German, British, and American military intervention (did you know that American troops also invaded our country?), we began to build our own military machine. There is no longer any secret about the fact that a tremendous proportion of scientific potential in my country is linked with defense work. The military sector of the economy receives the best brains, the best material resources, and operates the best technologies.

All that is the result of the arms race. It exhausts humanity as a whole and puts a great burden upon our economy. Being aware of the global senselessness of this process I can't help noticing one glaring contradiction. When I speak to military men I find them intelligent, kind, and calm people. Educated, too. They sincerely believe that what they are doing is something everybody needs. Therein lies a great problem, too. A moral problem, if you like. What is good and what is bad in a military unit, or in an army, or in the armed forces of the whole world? We have reached a point where what is bad for the world as a whole takes precedence over everything else. Some ten or twenty years ago we believed that what was bad for our country was something we had to watch out for. Today we understand that we absolutely must not do at all what is bad for the whole world. I think Sweden understood this sooner than other countries.

R E   The substance of the problem could be that both East and West are in the grip of the old type of thinking, which, in our present situation, looks more like madness.

A Y   It looks as if you were right.

R E   This sounds like a vicious circle. People are afraid. Fear leads to an arms race, and the arms race breeds new fear.

A Y   It also breeds poverty and the destruction of the natural environment.

R E Let's take Europe as an example, with its nuclear weapons stockpiles greater than in any other part of the world. Europe saw the start of the two greatest wars of our century. But does anybody seriously believe that small European countries will unleash a war against one another? After suffering the greatest losses in the history of mankind, run-down Europe learned its lessons. So the superpowers have located their nuclear bases in the heart of Europe for purposes other than keeping the irresponsible Europeans from setting fire to the powder keg.

A Y You don't seem to believe that Europe can start another war?

R E No, I don't. I even think that if Europe did not have nuclear weapons, no single European country would plan to acquire such weapons or ask the superpowers to station them on its territory.

Actually, I see no European problem that might explode into an armed conflict between the superpowers. It is difficult even to imagine that there is anyone in the East or in the West, any responsible political figure who would seriously believe that the other side can deliberately unleash a war.

Nevertheless the end of the world may come if the sides maintain the climate of distrust and continue to pile up weaponry. The very escalation of the arms race is fraught with this danger. Experience shows that sooner or later any new type of weapon is put to use. While we continue to play with cosmic forces, we put at risk, through some fateful negligence, the fruits of four billion years of evolution on our planet.

This is the logic of the arms race: when there is too little weaponry, they say, the situation is dangerous, while an excess of weapons allegedly makes the countries more secure. Both sides reason on the same lines, and this alone keeps the arms race going.

But the very idea that the other side threatens your security is a mere myth, and a terrible myth at that. What stands between John and Ivan who stand at their missile launchers on either side of the artificial dividing line, taking aim at each other? Nevertheless the myth exists and is in itself a source of danger.

Remember King Arthur's last battle. He and his knights gathered around the rough oaken table for peace talks. Suddenly one of them whipped out his sword. The others took it as a threat and also bared their swords and went for one another in an indiscriminate slaughter in which all of them died. But the first one took to arms because he had seen a snake on the floor. His intention had not been correctly understood.

A Y   And what happened to the snake?

R E   It may still be alive to this day.

A Y   To this day?

R E   Yes. In the sense that the measures taken by one side could easily be misinterpreted as aggressive where no aggression was meant.

In the final analysis, the main threat possibly comes not from the nuclear weapon as such, but from the new computerized military technology, where the weapons are less bulky and weighty, where they are more mobile and have great explosive power. This is also where the computer program of the rocket carrier contains data for hitting several targets accurately at a time. All this rapid development changes the very nature of risk itself.

The growing role of computers limits man's possibilities for observing the course of events and controlling them. The danger of a war being deliberately started may have lessened but the risk of an accidental flareup may well have increased. This madness is built into the very programs of computers. Just one mistake, one wrong conclusion made by the electronic brain, or a mere malfunction of a sensor may lead to irreversible consequences. With all these factors in mind, we cannot think in terms of the experience of the last century. This is plain dangerous.

The culmination of this dangerous development is militarization of outer space, something that has come to be known as "star wars."

A Y   But as the U.S. president has said, "star wars" are of a defensive character and are a high technology response to the development of nuclear weapons.

R E Defense!.. Don't you think that the sweeping plan for space defense
is fatalistic in the most dismal sense of the term? Because those who
are going to start militarization of outer space, to deploy so-called
defensive weapons there, clearly proceed from the assumption that
no practical disarmament will ever take place.

After all, even laser beams aimed at the enemy's missiles in outer
space can hit land-based targets. To hit a fast-flying missile is a
difficult task. Some experts even say that this would be impossible.
It has been calculated that the energy of a laser beam must be
100,000 times as great as the energy of a solar beam. It is all too
clear that to hit an immobile land-based target, these weapons do
not need to have such power and such accuracy. Laser beams directed from outer space (according to some experts) can within minutes cause a thousand fires on earth. Its effect would be the same as
that of a world nuclear war: a global winter night, except that it
would have no radioactive fallout.

The idea that some nation, on the threshold of the third millennium, has usurped the right to place, high up in the sky, a weapon
of this kind is both fantastic and outrageous. What kind of life
would there be for people, knowing that spacecraft equipped with
laser weapons are circling over their heads every minute of the day!
That would be psychological terrorism. And what can be considered to belong to all of us but the air we breathe?

A Y I quite agree with everything you're saying about "star wars." But
the question still remains. After all, what you've just said is well
known to the advocates of deployment of nuclear weapons in outer
space. In the United States, Japan, and other countries public opinion is divided between those who support and those who oppose
"star wars." Knowing how sophisticated and how hazardous modern
technology is, we can only wonder how cynical one may get to con-
template the possibility of "star wars." They even believe, just like
we do here, that actually no "star wars" are possible, but add that
the very preparations for such wars are merely a source of profit
already, today.

RE   It seems to me that many people get carried away by what new high technology has opened up for us, and give little thought to what practical uses it may have.

AY   However, we cannot help thinking about the future of our children and our grandchildren.

RE   It looks like they don't even bother asking themselves such questions. In many respects these men look very much like the military men you spoke about: they are intelligent, dignified, and even kind people. At the same time, their way of thinking is fully controlled by their profession. This is why they are lured by new possibilities offered by advanced modern technology. Many people are apprehensive that Europe may soon lose many of its most talented scientists and engineers who might be attracted by the prospects of some more daring and pioneering aspect of this project.

AY   So a science linked with militarism turns out to be more and more antihumane in its substance, doesn't it?

RE   Regrettably, this seems to be the case. And this is why we can conclude, in our dialogue, that the broad sections of the population of the world must take a deeply humanistic view and be aware of the dangers, their scope and substance, threatening us at every step.

AY   There is no custodian of absolute truth. We ourselves, our army generals, our political leaders are all human, and are therefore not immune from making errors. They can make both right and wrong decisions. However, what makes our epoch different from all others is that at the end of the twentieth century our decisions are responsible for the future of the world.

I remember that in the late 1950s the former Soviet leader, Nikita Khrushchev, entered into a heated debate with the Chinese leadership. The Chinese said then: "There may be an atomic war. And since there are more of us than any other people, we have a greater chance of survival, even if several hundred million Chinese vanished off the face of the Earth." When Khrushchev heard that, he said: "We don't need a communism bought at the price of millions of human lives." Khrushchev was right.

I think that the price that the world has to pay for ideological differences is becoming prohibitive. But the complexity of the world lies in the fact that it is not only ideology, and not only militarism that hold back the solution of our common problems. If we compare per capita national incomes in different countries, we shall see that in the developed countries this income is tens of times as high as it is in the developing countries. And, at the same time, as far as I know, the rate of armament is the highest in Africa. The point is that the poorest nations regard armament as the most effective way to solve all their problems. If we look at it from the other side, we shall see that the growing population is a serious problem in itself.

This is why it happens that ecological problems cannot be considered aside from political problems, nor can the political problems be discussed outside a discussion of ecological problems. I do not know all the answers to these questions, but I am convinced that it is not for politicians only to resolve them. Maybe in the future a world government will have to be formed to cope with all these tasks. We must think about it, and think now. Every country in the world must be represented in this government.

We said, among other things, that outer space belongs to us all. However, this holds true not only for outer space, but also for the air and water—not the World Ocean alone, but all water that comes down from the sky. Water also belongs to all. We shall come back to that later on. The conclusion that suggests itself is that this common property must be protected and that there is no one country in the world that can claim the right to control this property.

I am not a politician. I am a biologist. These questions concern me insofar as they are directly linked with ecology. Birds that multiply in my country then fly to other countries for the winter. There is a small bird that breeds in the Soviet Arctic and spends the winter in New Zealand. All countries of the world are linked among themselves and also with living nature. This ecological aspect of the problem prompts us to moot the question about the inevitability of the new political thinking.

Here is a simple example. There is a certain type of swan living in the tundra of the Yamal peninsula. In winter these birds migrate to Britain. There they live in special sanctuaries where the authorities take special measures to protect the swans during the wintering season. And if anyone attempted to build a new town in the place of some swamped-up estuaries, our tundras would soon lose all these swans. However, the swans are only the top of the ecological pyramid. All living things on earth are closely linked together. Every plant species is linked with tens of species of insects, and each bird species is linked with hundreds of species of invertebrates. If we lose the swan population, this means that Europe's natural environment will lose dozens of other living species. That would eventually act as a kind of ecological bomb just as terrible as the accident in Chernobyl. This is a serious problem.

Modern technology presents still another problem. On the one hand, it leads to the destruction of man. But can't we do anything so that modern technology could be used to destroy the means of destruction? Let's do a bit of dreaming. For example, would it be possible to develop a technology to destroy all nuclear warheads? On the other hand, new technology can produce still greater dangers than the nuclear weapon itself. For example, there are plans for reflecting light from outer space upon vast areas of our planet. This plan is quite realistic from the point of view of modern technology. A giant mirror made of some kind of film could be spread out in outer space to throw solar light upon a particular area of the globe. This might easily become an ecological weapon against plants and animals. Nothing would change except for the light, but that would disrupt all the existing physiological processes. This is just one example, among many others.

I just cannot see clear-cut answers to these questions. But the very fact that they have been raised at all is very symptomatic indeed.

DAY

2

THE WHOLE WORLD KNOWS OF OUR
PROGRAM ... FOR RENOUNCING NUCLEAR WAR.
I AM TRYING TO UNDERSTAND WHY THE WESTERN
POWERS DO NOT SUPPORT US IN THIS ENDEAVOR.
THE ONLY PLAUSIBLE EXPLANATION I CAN FIND
IS THAT THEY DO NOT TRUST US.

—ALEXEI YABLOKOV

THE WEST, TOO, IS APPREHENSIVE ABOUT THE
SOVIET UNION AND ITS INTENTIONS. YOU
YOURSELF HAVE MENTIONED THE STALIN
PERIOD, ... THE CONSEQUENCES OF WHICH YOU
ARE ELIMINATING. YOU CAN'T GET AWAY FROM
THE FACT THAT THE IMAGE OF YOUR COUNTRY
AT THAT TIME WAS VERY GRIM, AND THAT THAT
IMAGE PROVED TO BE TENACIOUS.

—ROLF EDBERG

■

RE Towards the end of our talk last night you spoke about the migratory birds that in winter fly off to New Zealand from your north, and about the swans that fly away to Britain where they spend the winter in special bird sanctuaries set up by British scientists. These birds are part of the beautiful world which we want so much to preserve.

But the first condition for making our planet fit for the life of migratory birds, of swans, also for the life of people, is to protect it from nuclear war. All types of nuclear weapons must be destroyed so that the globe can remain the abode of all life.

Many people think that we have a chance to make history in achieving this, that we have a possibility for a fresh start after the leaders of the superpowers agreed to rid the world of nuclear weapons. Gorbachev's idea of a nuclear-free world in the year 2000 has given people hope for the future. But after so many hopes have collapsed, when one sees that representatives of the superpowers find it difficult to come to terms on ordinary procedural matters, many people naturally ask themselves if these new hopes are at all realistic. And yet, after so many years of fear, disappointment, and the cold war, the first steps are being taken. Although the decisions made so far are of no consequence from the military point of view, we still hope that their political, symbolic role will prove to be of much greater importance.

How do you, Alexei, view this from your vantage point on the banks of the Moskva River?

A Y I think that the world has finally matured for the new political thinking of which Albert Einstein and Bertrand Russell said back in 1955 in their Manifesto: "Remember your humanity, and forget the rest."

All political leaders have made many statements that nuclear war is impossible. American, European, and Asian politicians are becoming more and more convinced that to start nuclear war would be suicidal. At the same time there are various points of view on how to avoid such a war. I feel very much concerned that in our world—both among communists and capitalists—there are influential politicians who think in terms of the policy of nuclear deterrent. We are told that the Second World War has been followed by forty plus years of peace precisely because of the existence of the atomic bomb, also because both sides have it. From my point of view this position is illogical. We say in this country that once a year a shotgun shoots by itself. Today the world has such enormous nuclear weapons stockpiles that they can "shoot" purely by accident.

The whole world knows of our program for renouncing nuclear weapons testing, for renouncing nuclear war. I am trying to understand why the western powers do not support us in this endeavor. The only plausible explanation I can find is that they do not trust us, even when we propose that on-site inspections be carried out on both sides. We are not trusted even when scientists say that there are very accurate facilities to detect nuclear blasts, like those in the house you told me about. Not trusted even when the Academy of Sciences of the USSR invites American observer teams to come to our testing grounds.

There must be a reason for this mistrust. To understand this reason let's take a look into the past. For a long time we also did not trust and still do not trust fully the military and political figures of the West. It is not our troops that were in America but American troops that invaded our country. My country, in this century alone, was twice attacked by Germany. I think it is easy to understand our apprehension and our mistrust. What would you say about that, Rolf?

RE Judging from what you say, your country has a deeply entrenched fear of foreign intervention. If I am not mistaken, the problem lies not in czarism or communism but in your historical experience.

May I ask you to tell me more in detail about the historical reasons why the Soviet Union feels encircled and is afraid of foreign invasion?

AY About a thousand years ago, when we were under pressure from the Tartar-Mongols, and the Russian state was in its infancy, it played an important role in preventing them from invading the whole of Europe. If that had happened, Europe would have been thrown whole centuries back in its development. Later, again for centuries, Russia was under threat not from the East, but from the West. In 1812, for example, Napoleon invaded Russia after he had conquered practically the whole of Europe. But here, in Russia, he got bogged down and lost his army. There were many other such invasions—from Poland, Lithuania, Sweden. But it seems that the turning point in Russia's history was the emergence of a socialist state on its territory in 1917. The event alarmed the capitalist world, which has ever since been putting pressure on Soviet Russia. This pressure acquired a political hue. The capitalist governments did not, from the very beginning, want Russia to exist as a socialist state.

It is true that our state has made many mistakes in the course of its development. The horrors of the Stalin regime, the flirtation with Hitler, and some steps taken by the Soviet Union in Europe had put the western world on its guard. And this is what I have in mind when I speak about the roots of mistrust toward my country.

RE I presume we can continue to talk about it frankly and without reserve. I think that before we continue the dialogue, we should try to clear up these questions for ourselves.

You are right, Alexei, in saying that the West does not have a clear idea, that, for historical reasons, the Soviet Union has that innate mistrust, that it is apprehensive of military intervention because it feels surrounded on all sides. However, it is necessary to understand the fact that the West, too, is apprehensive of the Soviet Union and its intentions. You yourself have mentioned the Stalin period, the period of terror and despotism, the consequences of which you are eliminating. You cannot get away from the fact that the image of your country at that time was very grim, and that that image proved to be tenacious. This general feeling was exacerbated after the unprovoked attack by the Soviet Union on Finland in 1939.

After the Second World War two events greatly helped strengthen this fear and mistrust. First, the coup in Czechoslovakia in 1948. People in the West feared that the Soviet Union would start subjugating one country after another all the way to the shores of the Atlantic. Of course, those apprehensions were greatly overblown, but still they were there. There is nothing accidental about the fact that the defense organization of NATO was set up a year after the events in Prague. And later almost incredible events occurred in 1961: the line of political division in Central Europe that had replaced the demarcation line drawn at the end of the war took the physical shape of the Wall where people were shot on sight for merely trying to cross over to the West. And, fair enough, Afghanistan which has become just as much a burden for the Soviet Union as Vietnam was for the United States.

In the West they can name a number of reasons why they should be afraid of the Soviet Union. At the same time people in the West know very little about what has caused the Soviet Union to fear the western blocs. I think the same situation obtains in the East: people fear the West but they do not understand why the West should fear the Soviet Union.

I think we have every right to say that the negative attitudes to one another have grown into dogmas. I believe it most important that the East and West should view each other from a different angle.

Those who knew the conditions and psychological make-up of the other side had for too long been denied access to the halls where crucial political decisions were made. I think that certain fatefully wrong judgments could have been avoided if the two sides had heeded those who had expert knowledge of the other side. Mistrust brought forth uncertainty, and this produced pretexts for threats.

AY I agree. That's the way it has always been. Our knowledge of each other is poor, and that's where our mistrust and many of our troubles come from. Now we could, just as frankly, discuss specific reasons for such mistrust. But maybe we shouldn't and just leave it to the historians. I could recall the events in Czechoslovakia and Hungary. In Hungary, in 1956, some ten thousand communists were hanged from the lampposts, and we just could not allow the death of tens of thousands more. You can criticize us, but you must agree that we cannot be blamed indiscriminately. There were also the events in Czechoslovakia known as the Prague Spring held to the rumbling of our tanks in the streets of Czechoslovak cities in 1968. Harking back to those days, people told this joke. "The changes in the leadership and policy of the Soviet Union in 1985 prompted the Czechoslovaks to decide whether the time has come for the Warsaw Treaty Organization to send troops to Moscow."

RE You say that in 1956, ten thousand communists were hanged, which is what caused the Soviet Union to intervene. I hear this figure for the first time, and this interpretation of the events is, I think, fairly wide of the mark. After the dramatic events in the autumn of 1956 the United Nations set up a commission, which included representatives of small countries from different parts of the world. In its report the commission declared that the Soviet tanks entered Budapest and opened fire in its streets because the people as a whole demanded freedom of speech, free elections, and a government headed by a pro-Tito communist, Imre Nagy, and because the Hungarians asked the United Nations to act in support of the idea of a neutral Hungary. Precisely the same way, eleven years later Soviet tanks entered Prague when, during the so-called Prague Spring, Alexander Dubcek and his government tried to put through something like what you call perestroika today.

AY I am quite positive that never once since the Second World War has the Soviet Union even thought of encroaching upon the established boundaries in Europe. In 1987 all the Warsaw Treaty countries made a solemn declaration, in the form of a military doctrine, that they had no territorial claims and that they would never start a war first. There is a lot more to be said in this respect.

I would like to focus on one important idea that you touched upon in our dialogue: the image of the enemy and who benefits from it. At the Moscow forum in the spring of 1987 West German scientist Sommer said that the image of the external enemy helps the government to stay away from the internal problems of the country. Sometimes we, undoubtedly, use this logic, too. I am sure that the Western governments also resort to this line of reasoning. All countries have many domestic problems, which the governments are reluctant to talk about.

This is not just lack of trust or a poor knowledge of history, but a deliberate enemy image-making, something we cannot dismiss out of hand. I remember very well the propaganda campaign launched in my country against so-called cosmopolitanism. In the 1950s, we isolated ourselves, if you like, by declaring that everything outside our borders, or outside the borders of our friends, was bad. And that was the atmosphere in which Soviet youth were brought up for about fifteen years. And today these same people who were educated in this manner are at the helm of our state.

It takes tremendous political wisdom to cut loose from the clutches of the external enemy image. I think that in the USSR we have come to the conclusion on all main levels that it is necessary to break away from this sort of image-building. This new attitude has become deeply entrenched in the minds of our intelligentsia, our workers and farmers. I am glad that it has extended to the very top of our government, too. Our society is now actively emancipating itself morally, ridding itself of the tragic mistakes of Stalinism as well as from the demoralizing, putrefying climate of many years of stagnation. There are still many facts unknown to us, and many archives are still closed to the public. It looks as if we shall yet have to go through a lot of things to cleanse our communist ideals from rot and filth.

I believe in the power of glasnost, in perestroika. At the same

time I see the difficulties that will have to be overcome to ensure
success. However, all these sore and at times tragic problems in the
life of our country cannot blot out the main thing: our awareness
that all countries must live together. How is this to be achieved? It
is clear that we must live in peace, without nuclear war, without
any war. We must also work together to cope with the global ecological crisis, and do it as soon as possible.

RE Regrettably, this ignorance is, in all probability, on both sides, so
that both must make the effort to see themselves through the eyes
of their counterpart and size up the situation as it really is. In order
that genuine disarmament might be possible, it seems necessary to
make a thorough study of some of the psychological factors and free
ourselves from the shadows of the past. To make substantial progress in military disarmament, we would have to get rid of the image
of the enemy.

I need a dialogue, a frank and free exchange of views in all
fields. Such dialogues should take place alongside unilateral measures taken by states in political and military spheres, alongside the
official negotiations in Geneva and at other international forums. To
my mind, human contacts and an exchange of thoughts and ideas
between representatives of different systems are very important.

I also think that the purely schematic division of the world into
communist and capitalist is oversimplified. I would not say outright that the mixed economy of the countries of northern Europe
is capitalist; we here tend to speak about the "third way." A modi-
cum of mixed economy can be detected in the communist countries, too.

There has been a lot said about peaceful coexistence. Wasn't it
Khrushchev who gave currency to this concept? Today, if we really
want to solve our problems, we cannot confine ourselves to peaceful
coexistence alone. What we need is fruitful and creative cooperation.

AY I agree with you. Let's try and think about what could be done now
in order to pass from mere coexistence to cooperation. We shall later

speak more in detail about what I call socialization of nature. I think that in some capitalist countries, such as Sweden or Italy, some aspects of the social attitude to nature are no less socialist than in our country. In this sense the boundary line between the capitalist and socialist approaches to the natural environment is somehow blurred. There is always a clear-cut boundary line between ideologies, but the boundary line between the way nature is used in different countries is another matter. We shall perhaps talk about it later, while now we shall try to set forth what exactly must be done in order to pass on from cool coexistence to mutual cooperation in the solution of ecological problems.

But before we get down to it I would like to support the idea of contacts between people and not just between professional politicians. Sometimes we can prompt politicians to elaborate further on their ideas. I'd like to recall here that Albert Einstein and Sigmund Freud had that approach back in the 1930s. On the eve of the Second World War they sought to find ways of avoiding a new war. So they came to this conclusion: it is necessary that the belligerent, feuding countries should engage in major joint projects. Modern technology gives us tremendous new possibilities in this direction. The American astrophysicist Carl Sagan has suggested that the Soviet Union and the United States undertake a joint Soviet-American flight to Mars. One cosmonaut would be a man and the other a woman. One American and the other Russian. The long months of the space journey would symbolize our joint efforts in the study of the universe. There would be many thousands of people wishing to take part in this project. It would no doubt serve to unite our planet Earth.

To my mind this project is not so fantastic as it sounds. Both American and Soviet scientists are dreaming about flying to Mars. Their joint efforts would technically facilitate bringing it about, which would also make a tremendous political impact. This project was formulated in 1987 and was supported by Soviet scientists. I sincerely hope that our government will uphold it, too.

Another example. In 1987, the International Physicians for the Prevention of Nuclear War put forward the idea of sending up a special communications satellite that would link doctors in the developing countries with doctors in the USSR and the United States so that any medical man in any developing country could promptly get professional advice from the best physicians of the world. I am glad that Mikhail Gorbachev has supported this proposal and said that our country will provide an artificial earth satellite for this purpose.

Third example. The calamity alarm system, which has been in operation for some time and which has helped save many lives in America and in other countries. This is the way that our countries, with widely differing political systems can step-by-step come together.

Another way is to find the means of better understanding human psychology. Very often Soviet people are accused of being unapproachable and incommunicative. This shows that the critics in the West simply do not understand our conditions. For example, I know that my American colleagues reproach the USSR because many areas of the country are closed to foreign visitors. Recently, I read a newspaper item which said, with references to the Intourist Travel Agency, that only 10 percent of the territory here is closed to foreigners. I can say for sure that many areas are off limits not because there is anything secret about them, but because we are embarrassed about showing them to foreigners, also because we often have no halfway decent hotels (or no hotels at all) and because our WCs are so dirty. A friend of mine, a professor from Novosibirsk, organized a joint Soviet-American expedition across the Republic of Kazakhstan and the Altai region. The only document required in order to obtain permission for the Americans to take part in this trip was a statement that they would agree to live outside cities and that they would not ask for hotel accommodations. Today one of the participants in this expedition has become the director of the famous Smithsonian Institution in Washington. He says he brought back home wonderful memories of a lifetime of that expedition.

RE Of course, the project of a joint flight to Mars by Soviet and American astronauts defies the imagination, as much as the project set forth by the Organization of International Physicians for the Prevention of Nuclear War. I agree that this undertaking would be of great symbolic and psychological significance. This may help unite us citizens of the Earth across ideological boundaries.

Let's not forget about our earthly problems that still await a solution and that must not be put off until the day when an American and a Russian set foot on Mars together. Why not, for example, "alongside the talks between the superpowers and between the military blocs about stage-by-stage disarmament, and regardless of these negotiations" step up the efforts to create nuclear-free zones? Every region of the globe freed from nuclear weapons can by rights be considered a contribution to relaxation of political tensions.

A short time ago I visited the South Pacific in order to see at first hand the creation of a nuclear-free zone by thirteen states. The work got off to a good start and was making fast progress. The decision to declare this area nuclear-free (very symbolic) was made in 1985, on the day of the fortieth anniversary of the Hiroshima tragedy. Now this agreement has come into force and will be effective over the vast region of the Pacific from the equator down to the Antarctic, except for "French" Polynesia where France continues with her nuclear testing on Mururua atoll. South America has also declared itself a nuclear-free zone. Antarctica is not subject to militarization in view of an international agreement to this effect.

Thus access to nuclear weapons is closed over a vast area of the globe. The number of such nuclear-free zones must be increased. Many people want to see Europe also turned into such a zone.

But there will be little use in setting up new nuclear-free zones and dismantling missile launchers on land if the funds thus released are used to develop naval armaments. The oceans are not free from nuclear weapons. The dark abyss is the borderline zone between peace and war where American and Soviet submarines carrying atomic weapons "feel each other out," acting with a fair degree of independence. Ordinary people are not informed of what is going on, nor are political leaders fully in control of these submarines' operations.

They sail in the ocean which the United Nations has proclaimed to be the property of all mankind. It seems that these submarines have the run of the place in neutral waters, too. In Sweden we are in possession of irrefutable evidence that foreign submarines are clearly in the habit of making themselves comfortable in the skerries and bays of Sweden.

I shall not go into these incidents any further, for the question at issue is a small fraction of the large-scale naval strategy which should be brought to light as fully as possible.

Since we think we can reach the planet Mars, which is fine of course, let's also take a look down below into the seas and oceans of our own planet.

A Y Every time I went to Sweden I was invariably asked about Soviet submarines.

R E You said "Soviet." All I said was foreign submarines.

A Y Many of my Swedish colleagues, experts in zoology, were greatly alarmed just as you are now. There are grounds for this feeling of apprehension. I saw a picturebook containing photographs of a Soviet submarine that had surfaced in Swedish waters. But when I asked about other similar cases the reply was at the level that someone had heard something somewhere underwater. However, when such would-be noises were examined, nothing was found (except maybe submarines from the NATO countries). So it seems that your real alarm stems from that one and only outrageous incident when our submarine had strayed into Swedish waters from its course and found itself stranded in a surface position. According to our official version, the submarine had lost its orientation. I know that this official Soviet version is treated in Sweden with a grain of salt.

But here we come up against a problem which concerned not only submarines but the behavior of the military in a broader context. Actually, their behavior is less predictable than one might expect. Here is an example. My brother, a marine geologist, worked in the Far East, in the Sea of Okhotsk, on a ship that prospected for minerals not far away from shore. Once when they were lying at anchor and doing their work because of poor visibility from fog, their ship was literally rammed by a naval vessel. When the incident was examined, it turned out that the naval vessel, if it had followed the charts, would have been several kilometers inside our territory, far away from the sea!

Regrettably, some individual army units may get out of control, and their discipline may be lax. And how many times did the American press publish reports about the sale of weapons and hardware worth hundreds of millions of dollars? I believe that our submarine could get lost in Swedish skerries, but I do not believe that our military experts want to ferret out any great secrets from the Swedes.

But if this is some kind of insidious strategy of Soviet admirals "to hide in the waters of neutral Sweden" as my Swedish friends have told me, then I cannot consider this strategy acceptable by any standards. You may be sure, many people in the Soviet Union share my skepticism about the statements by Swedish military authorities on the alleged invasion of Swedish waters by our submarines. The Swedish defense ministry has announced that in the summer of 1986 alone, foreign (implying Soviet!) submarines intruded into Swedish waters thirty times. Our press even published satirical articles about that announcement!

I can add here that on the whole, Soviet people trust Sweden more than many other western countries. Perhaps no small part of this trust is owing to the fine quality of your Volvo cars.

Now a few more words about the sea. This theme is very close to my heart, as I have spent my whole life studying marine mammals. I visited the southern and northern seas, studied marine animals on the coasts of California and Chukotka, in the Baltic and Greenland seas. To me the very idea that our seas are "teeming" with nuclear submarines carrying warheads of monstrous destructive power is especially repugnant.

The last Congress of Soviet writers heard an interesting discussion between an author and a representative of the Soviet general staff. The author had written a story about the captain of a nuclear submarine. In this story the author puts this question to the captain: "How do you feel knowing that the fate of the whole world is in your hands?" The captain replies: "Since the world is built that way, somebody must do the job I am doing!" The author queries: "And if you find out that the enemy has attacked your country and in fact has destroyed it, would you press the button to destroy that enemy? You must understand that your action would be senseless!" The captain replies: "May no one know what I shall do." This reply aroused the displeasure of our general, the one who represented the General Staff. I think that this general typifies the old and by now obsolete doctrine of nuclear retaliation.

It is no secret that the USSR has a powerful fleet of nuclear submarines. And again, one must look back over the years in order to understand the position of my country. The Soviet Union is surrounded by United States military bases on all sides. Wherever you look—west, south or east—you see U.S. military bases. Just one look at the map of these bases makes you feel uneasy . . .

I can understand our military experts who some thirty years ago decided that the only protection against such encirclement would be submarines that can lie on the sea floor for months waiting for an order. They are capable of sending missiles to any part of the globe. This is the terrible reality of the modern world that I cannot bear thinking about!

Is there any way of relieving the ocean of this burden? If this is to be done, the success can come only from the joint efforts of the whole world. For us in the Soviet Union, one thing is clear—we shall never start a nuclear war first!

RE Let's not start a bilateral discussion about submarines entering Swedish territorial waters. This is a matter for our foreign ministries. There are only two remarks I would like to make. First, it would be very difficult to convince the Swedes, who know the skerries off Karlskrona, that the submarine you mentioned ran aground due to a navigational error. Secondly, it is hardly appropriate to call all the instances of detection of foreign submarines in our territorial waters chimerical. Of course, there are reports whose veracity is doubtful, as always happens in such cases. However, there are many convincing facts, too. We failed to identify the country to which the submarines belonged but in one case a special commission headed by a former foreign minister established that the intruder belonged to the Warsaw Treaty Organization.

But, as I said, this is just a detail, and a minor detail at that, in a big naval strategy. This is a kind of cat-and-mouse game that the superpowers are playing in the ocean depths. This game is very worrisome. A short time ago the foreign minister of Sweden, Sten Andersson, made a public statement that the risk of a nuclear weapon being used is particularly great in the ocean. In a crucial situation someone might easily be tempted to use the nuclear weapon mounted on a submarine in order to sink an enemy aircraft carrier. Supposing one has crossed the nuclear threshold, what would be the next step?

What is going on underwater is not just a matter for the super-powers. This concerns all nations insofar as the ocean is common property.

You spoke about the fear inspired by the U.S. bases. This fear is not only on your side, but on both sides. In the West people are also frightened! What is necessary is to remove the mutual feeling of threat, no matter where this threat comes from—from land-based missiles, from outer space, or from the ocean depths. And this is where politics and intellect are closely interwoven. Standing behind all weapons are people, human beings with their fears, their mis-trust, prejudice, and biased opinions.

And again we come to the conclusion that in our atomic age we need the new thinking. It looks as if it is easier to get rid of obsoles-cent technology than to find new ways of thinking.

A Y Yes, all changes should begin in our minds when it comes to mis-trust. I have spoken with hundreds of people in different coun-tries—Americans, Swedes, British, Czechoslovaks, Poles. Of all those people there was only one man who was aggressive towards the USSR. That was in Kraków, Poland. It was late when I went into a cafe. Sitting across the table from me was a slightly drunken

Pole. We fell to talking about something. When he learned that I was Russian, he blurted out: "We shall take the Ukraine away from you so that Poland will again stretch from sea to sea." I'd like to add, by way of explanation, that there was a period in history, I think it was in the seventeenth century, when Poland's borders stretched from the Baltic Sea to the Black Sea.

I am quite convinced that the United States does not want to attack my country, nor does my country want to attack the United States.

RE There have been lots of official statements made by Soviet and American leaders to the effect that their two nations are not going to attack one another. Nevertheless, the two are spending staggering sums on defense against possible attack. All that an observer from a small neutral country can say is that one side should make an all-out effort to convince the other of the sincerity of these assurances. The present phase of detente, which came after a quarter of a century of fruitless negotiations, should be used to build up a climate of trust, and do this wisely, stage by stage.

I would like to dwell on a question that seems to play no small role, either. This has to do with the part of Europe west of the Soviet Union, the area between the Arctic Ocean, the Atlantic Ocean, and the Mediterranean Sea. This region is a mosaic of peoples who speak fifty or so languages and are divided into thirty states. There is undoubtedly, however, some sort of inner connection between all of them. In spite of the differences between them, and in spite of their many political systems, these states could well maintain normal relations in a spirit of cooperation were it not for the existence of political blocs.

This part of Europe will never be able to become a union, a state formation, something like the United States or the Soviet Union. However, it would be quite possible to develop closer cooperation between its various parts in economic, technological and ecological fields.

Western Europe is a region where cooperation is becoming closer and more extensive. Plans are afoot for signing an agreement on free trade, which will cover not only the EEC but also the neutral states which, for military and political motives, have not joined the Common Market. Also planned is the free movement of commodities, services, people and capital. Cooperation in the fields of science and high technology is developing within the framework of an organization called Eureka, which is expected, among other things, to stop the brain drain from Western Europe. Many other interesting projects are also on the drawing board.

You have just spoken about the possibility of Soviet-American cooperation in outer space. In Western Europe thirty nations have formed the European Space Agency in order that Europe should not fall behind in space exploration which may be of such importance for industrial development. Also underway is cooperation in the physics of fundamental particles. Such alliances in different fields which may be called "interest federations" may facilitate the development of something new, something that will fuse the multitude of elements of that part of the world into one whole.

Hence my question: would it not be reasonable and useful if the countries of eastern Europe also joined together in some forms of cooperation which are taking shape in western Europe? They might very well gain by it even more than western Europe.

The idea I am trying to get across is that expansion of such cooperation would make this region more independent and self-sufficient. This is particularly important since western Europe serves as a buffer zone between the two superpowers which have no common border.

Willy Brandt has outlined the contours of Europeanization that would gradually weaken control by the superpowers over their respective halves of Europe.

As a European from a country situated far up in the north I think that a Europe free from blocs could be an independent force between the existing poles of power. To my mind this would further ease relations and could, in the long run, serve the national interests of the superpowers, too.

What would you say to that, Alexei, as an individual and as a citizen of one of the superpowers?

AY I am not a specialist on the questions you have touched upon. As a matter of fact I have never given much thought to it. It seems to me, though, that not just political, but economic problems will create a serious drag on our "unification" with the countries of western Europe. Just think: our rubles, like Polish zlotys, and Czechoslovak korunas, and Bulgarian levs, are not convertible. Of course, economics and politics are closely interwoven here.

On the other hand, I see many ways of strengthening cooperation between European countries. I believe there are no serious obstacles here for technological cooperation. And although on the whole Western industry is more advanced (I say that as a layman), I have heard that we also have many technological projects that the West might find interesting.

There is still another sphere of beneficial cooperation. What I have in mind is protection of migratory animals, and especially birds and bats. We have no agreements on the protection of migratory birds with European countries, where such birds stop for a rest during their seasonal migrations. And how well it would be to build up such natural ecological contacts between countries and set them down in formal agreements. And this is quite realistic, a lot more realistic than making the Soviet ruble into a convertible currency.

RE I have a lot to say about the problems you have raised. However, I think I should leave it until later. The important thing is that western Europe can have a balancing effect on relations between the superpowers. It is necessary to facilitate the links between the European countries and to establish a dialogue between western Europe and the Soviet Union!

AY It seems to me that this would be no easy job to do. I can imagine Scandinavia as one whole, but I cannot imagine the same for the whole of Europe. There are too many differences between Britain, West Germany, Italy, Portugal, Bulgaria, Poland, and so on, in cultural and economic matters, even in the standards of behavior of their citizens. If I were a politician I would make an unqualified statement in support of the independence of Europe as an entity, just like Japan, the United States, and the Soviet Union are today. But now it seems that some western European states will yet for a long time be heeding recommendations from the United States.

In other words, I wish all the best to United Europe.

RE I am very pleased that you are so willing to join in the building of a more independent Europe, which may not necessarily be united, though more so than it is today.

I would like to go back to our conversation about nuclear energy. After all, it is used not only for military but also for peaceful purposes. Once the slogan "atom for peace" was very popular. However, the use of nuclear energy is not all that beneficial to society as was once thought.

Each link in the nuclear chain is harmful to the environment in one way or another. Already the first such link—the mining of uranium ore—produces poisonous wastes. Then comes enrichment with its hazards of radioactive contamination. And finally, the third link is the fissure of nuclei in the reactors of atomic-power stations. Chernobyl, a town in the Ukraine, which was little known outside the USSR, has become a symbol just as nuclear weapons had made Hiroshima and Bikini symbolic many years ago.

What happened in Chernobyl was neither new, nor unexpected. That was simply the twenty-seventh recorded major accident at nuclear-power stations since the time when the first power station of this type went into service in Obninsk, in the USSR. Very possibly, this is not the last, and possibly not the worst such accident. While we use nuclear energy no accident of this kind can be ruled out. The specific feature of Chernobyl is that clouds of radioactive cesium spread out much farther away from the source than had then been thought possible. And the very fact that reindeer in Sweden and sheep in Scotland have to be slaughtered because their food—grass and lichen—contains too much cesium gives more proof that nuclear-power stations are not just a matter for the countries that build them.

And finally, the fourth link seems to be much more dangerous than nuclear reactor accidents. I mean the growing stocks of nuclear waste which, contrary to assurances, people have not yet learned how to neutralize. There are very stable isotopes. If you take strontium, for example, it has many isotopes whose half-decay period is fairly short, whereas these periods of other isotopes may be as long as ten million years. I think it's humiliating even to think that we will leave all that radioactive waste behind for future generations to dispose of.

A Y I am afraid that when it comes to atomic energy we shall have a duet, and not a dialogue. All I can do is to add something to what you have already said.

Most nuclear energy specialists are trying to convince us that it is the most ecologically pure type of energy. To back up their claims they cite many figures illustrating the incidence of cancer and other diseases that are a lot higher when conventional fuels such as oil, gas, and coal are used.

We also hear nuclear physicists say that the hazard of accidents at modern nuclear-power stations is negligible. But Chernobyl clearly showed up the groundlessness of such assurances. Today there are about four hundred nuclear-power stations in twenty-six countries, all of which account for about 10 percent of the total amount of electricity produced. In some countries, such as France, almost 30 percent of the energy is generated at nuclear-power stations. However, I heard other considerations, too. If a mere 10 percent of the money used on the development of nuclear power engineering had been channeled into the development of alternative technologies, we would have no need for NPSs at all.

It has been said that there are plans for the building of as many as 20,000 NPSs throughout the world. Here in front of me is a diagram showing the evolution of public opinion after the accidents in Three Mile Island and Chernobyl. In 1976, 60 percent of the population of the United States were tolerant of the development of NPSs. After the Three Mile Island accident this figure dropped to 40 percent, and after Chernobyl to a mere 20 percent. This is a fact that neither politicians nor technicians can ignore.

On my last flight to Sweden our airplane stopped over at Copenhagen. The giant windmills of Danish electric power stations standing in open fields are very impressive indeed. Their gigantic slow-turning blades inspire a feeling of respect and security.

Of course, we should look for other ecologically and politically safer sources of energy than nuclear ones. Incidentally, I heard that superconductivity will help save a lot of energy. And in general there are vast power-saving reserves in the world. Maybe we don't need NPSs at all!

RE You say that thousands of new NPSs may be built in the future. For my part I am convinced that they will never be built.

"The dragon is dead, but only he doesn't know about it," said an American researcher ten or so years ago. The attitude to NPSs that you mentioned just now is getting increasingly negative. In the United States orders for the building of a hundred such stations have been canceled, and over the past ten years not a single new order has been made. In France where resistance to NPSs is not so strong as in the other countries of western Europe, 50 percent of those polled think that the use of nuclear energy is too hazardous. The Swedish parliament has ruled to dismantle all the NPSs in our country by the year 2010, and the job of dismantling is planned to start in the mid-1990s.

Incidentally, there is a military side to the peaceful uses of nuclear energy. The thing is that the plutonium obtained at NPSs can be used in nuclear weapons, too. Peaceful nuclear energy is a cousin to military nuclear energy.

You are speaking about nuclear power as a fait accompli. And really, in spite of negative public opinion, there are hundreds of operating NPSs; in some countries of the East, plans are afoot for the building of power stations. This, however, is a reversible process. We have proved that we can build NPSs. But we can also dismantle them, as we can nuclear weapons.

You have mentioned pure sources of energy coming from nature itself. It could be that early in the next century we shall learn how to use some of these inexhaustible sources. We have solved the problem of obtaining hydrogen by splitting up molecules of water. Gaseous hydrogen could heat apartments and could set cars in motion; putting it in a simpler form, our cars could run on water, instead of petrol. The idea is to design dependable, foolproof reservoirs. Work is underway to study this problem.

New, although so far not altogether perfect, ways of transforming solar energy into electricity have been found. The Soviet Union has built its first helioelectric power stations near the Sea of Azov, and is planning, as far as I know, to build an installation twenty times as powerful in Uzbekistan.

But I agree with you, Alexei: we must make far greater efforts to develop alternative sources. Speaking about atomic energy we can say that we have started playing with cosmic forces, having neither moral maturity nor deep enough knowledge to cope with it.

DAY
3

SOMETIMES I FIND MYSELF HATING MY SCIENCE,
BECAUSE IT GIVES ME KNOWLEDGE THAT ALMOST
MAKES ME WEEP.

—ALEXEI YABLOKOV

WE HAVE CITED MANY FIGURES AND WILL MOST
LIKELY CITE MANY MORE. BUT LET'S DRY OUR
TEARS AND TRY TO SEE HUMAN BEINGS
BEHIND THE STATISTICS.

—ROLF EDBERG

■

RE We have spent two days talking about the nuclear menace. But even if all nuclear weapons were destroyed mankind would still be living under a grave threat of another kind. It is obvious that we are rapidly moving towards an ecological disaster, if we continue to treat our planet so outrageously, that is. For my part I see at least three major ecological hazards that are different but closely linked to one another.

First, the growing anthropogenic pressure upon the globe, and its limited resources. The main thing here is the inordinate growth of the population itself. Second, the prodigal waste of the mined materials. And, finally, the third hazard, which is the destruction and contamination of everything that makes life possible. All that constitutes no lesser threat to the future of mankind than the nuclear weapon.

If, in the search for an Ariadne's thread in this vast labyrinth, we start out with the population explosion, I think, Alexei, you have something important to say, since you take special interest in this problem.

AY I sure have, Rolf. But before I get down to any specific figures and other data, I would like to illustrate the main theses you mentioned. Otherwise it will not be clear why we should worry about the growing size of the world population.

Today the average per capita amount of minerals mined annually throughout the world is twenty tons. Every citizen of our planet throws away one ton of garbage every year. About half the surface of the Earth has already been modified by man, with 11 to 12 percent of this area ploughed up, 25 to 27 percent taken up with other farm fields and plantations. The total area taken up by roofs and roads is greater than the territory of France.

The ocean that we have so much spoken about has become a regular rubbish bin whose dimensions defy the imagination: for every square kilometer of the oceanic surface an average of seventeen tons of garbage is dumped into the water every year. We shall speak about water in more detail further in this account. All I want now is to cite just one figure. Before reaching the ocean the water of the Thames River passes through the human organism seven to eight times. And now a few words about agriculture. One large livestock farm pollutes the environment as would a city with a population of 100,000.

All this shows that anthropogenic pressure upon the environment has grown to almost unimaginable proportions. The reason is that the population is growing very rapidly. There are too many of us in the world already. In July 1987 humanity passed another milestone in its history: its size reached a mammoth five billion. According to some forecasts, the population will continue to grow in the future. Demographers say that in some fifty years the population may double its present size. But if this is so, how will our planet stand up to all that? Why is this growth continuing? And what should be the attitude of mankind to this phenomenon?

RE I was born early in this century, so I am getting on at seventy-six. I was born in . . .

AY . . . in 1912?

RE Exactly! At that time the population of the Earth was a mere 1.5 billion. But now, as you pointed out, the population is 5 billion. Since the day I was born the number of my traveling companions, so to speak, has increased by 3.5 billion. Our planetary home is getting more and more crowded, and in the future it will be even more so. You are twenty years my junior and you will live to see the year 2000 when the number of your traveling companions will have grown by another billion.

Even if the rate of population growth has somewhat gone down—primarily owing to the stringent family planning measures in densely populated China—it will continue to grow at an appalling speed. Every minute 250 children are born, every day the population of the earth grows by one quarter of a million, and over one year by 80 million, which is ten times the size of population in Sweden. According to a UN forecast, by the middle of the next century the population of the Earth will have grown to between 12 and 14 billion. It stands to reason that should this process continue, the consequences would be unpredictable.

The figures we've cited may give a still better idea of what is happening if we extrapolate them to individual continents and countries. The population of Africa is now 500 million people. At the present rate of growth (it doubles every twenty years), by the year 2050 it will reach the 4 billion mark, which is slightly less than the population of the globe today. In Nigeria the population is 95 million. There the population doubles every seventeen years. At this rate Nigeria's population will be 620 million by the year 2050. This means that the population of Nigeria will in that year be greater than the population of the whole of Africa today. But this cannot go on forever.

Every new citizen of the Earth needs food, shelter, clothing, and at least some kind of education. Every citizen needs his share of the social infrastructure.

Norwegian Prime Minister Gro Harlem Brundtland, Chairman of the UN World Commission on Environment and Development, has said that we must plan our future so that we can combine the two worlds in just one world. And this is true: in just half a century there may be twice as many people on Earth as today. But is this realistic?

A Y To better understand what we should do, we have to look back over a certain period. The population explosion that we can see in the world today is particularly apparent in the developing countries. A similar population explosion was taking place in the advanced countries some time ago. In those days the Earth was strong enough

to stand up to it. Today the advanced countries have zero population growth, and in some of them population growth is even negative. According to statistics, the size of the population in West Germany, for example, is shrinking. This drop in the birth rate is
largely due to better medical care, which ensures the almost full
survival of the newly born. Life expectancy has also increased markedly. In the advanced countries life expectancy is almost twice as
long as that in some developing countries. So I think the measures
being taken to limit the birthrate in China and in seventy-six other
countries may not be so effective after all as a natural course of
events, if we want to limit the size of the population.

A mere ten years ago very few people imagined that the population of the advanced countries would go down so rapidly. According
to some forecasts, by the end of the twenty-first century when the
population of the Earth has stabilized, the total population of Europe will be half of what it is today. The problem is that stabiliza-
tion of the population of the Earth may level off somewhere between
8 and 15 billion people. From the point of view of ecology, 15
billion would be too many. Eight billion would be more likely and
indeed more desirable. And these 8 billion must live in good conditions. However, even now when there are "a mere" 5 billion
people on Earth we cannot assure good conditions for all of us. Half
a billion people in the world are starving, 93 newborn babies out of
every 1,000 in developing countries die within one year. The quality of three-quarters of the housing in the world is below even the
most modest standards, one-third of the adult population in the
world is either fully or partially unemployed. There are more than
10 million refugees, people who have lost their homes and live in
other countries. All that speaks for the fact that our human house-
hold is very poorly managed, which poses very serious problems
already for the near future.

RE You have given very graphic examples illustrating the pressure
upon the Earth and its resources from the mounting population,
also from poverty which has afflicted a considerable part of humanity.

I would like to add one more example that is very much on my mind. This is South America, with its one million children abandoned by their parents because they just cannot support them. These children can be seen everywhere, eating whatever they can pick up on garbage heaps or in the streets. Isn't this evidence of the tremendous imbalance between what we call the industrially advanced countries and underdeveloped countries?

Two-thirds of the population of the globe have to put up with living standards that are a mere 5 to 10 percent of those maintained by the richest countries. A Swede, a Swiss, or a North American consumes forty times as much as a Somalian, counting all types of resources, and eats seventy-five times as much meat and meat products as an Indian.

A British journalist has calculated that a cat in Britain eats twice as much meat protein as an average African. What is more, the price of the food that this cat eats is higher than the per capita average income of one billion people in poor countries.

This imbalance is also reflected in what you mentioned earlier: people fleeing from one country to another. You put their number at 10 million. To my knowledge, there are 15 million of them. Whichever figure is more accurate, we're speaking about a vast army of despairing people who leave areas which have been ravaged by war and famine, about migration brought forth by poverty.

AY I would like to add here that according to statistics, in the United States 30 percent of all people of over forty years of age are overweight. In 1982, Britain spent $235 million on slimming as against $50 million spent in aid for starving people in other countries.

RE We have cited many figures and will most likely cite many more. But let's wipe off the tears and try to see people behind the statistics. This is what we have to do.

I'd like to speak about migration again. There is another kind of migration, more extensive and a lot more rapid than at any other time. What I have in mind is the migration from rural areas to

constantly growing cities. And here again Latin America provides a
graphic example, since migration there has assumed avalanche proportions. In 1930, the urban population there stood at 30 million,
whereas by the end of this century the number of city-dwellers,
which probably will have increased twenty times over, will be close
to 600 million. This concerns the already large cities that continue
to grow. This figure stands for people who have abandoned the depleted lands and set out for the oversized cities with a multi-million
population, with very slim hopes that they will ever be able to find
work there. They live in shantytowns, in the so-called underprivi-
leged areas stretching from the center of the city to the slums de-
void of even the most primitive sanitation facilities, medical care,
and schools, with staggering unemployment. How degrading it is
to man! And what new epidemics can these slums produce due to
the crowded conditions!

What can we expect if population growth continues, with more
and more millions flowing into cities which already now are unable
to cope with their growth problems.

A Y This situation in South America you are talking about with so
much anguish is truly awful! However, I would not agree with your
overall assessment of the urbanization process. It is true that early
in this century only 14 percent of the population lived in cities. In
1970 this figure had grown to 50 percent. According to some forecasts, 70 percent of the population of the earth will live in cities at
the end of this century. Does this happen owing to poverty alone?
There are objective, economic reasons for it.

In the past, most of the population of the world was engaged in
food production. Thanks to progress in agriculture, the advanced
industrial regions, such as the United States and Western Europe,
now have about 5 percent of their population living in rural areas
and actually providing the remaining 95 percent with agricultural
produce. At the same time in Africa, for example, 60 percent of the
population are engaged in agricultural production. In my own
country where farming is less developed than, say, in the United

States, 20 percent of the population are in agricultural production. If only 10 percent of the population could provide food for the whole of the USSR, given the right organization of agricultural production, the other 10 percent would then move to cities and towns in the near future. Herein, I think, lies the economic reason for the growth of cities.

In principle, urban life must afford man more comforts and more possibilities for contacts with culture, more possibilities for intellectual development. This does not always happen, it is true. In the shantytowns and favelaes (slums or tenements) that you just spoke about, the living conditions breed crime. Do people really come into this world in order to spend their lives in unacceptable living conditions? And this is where we have come to this philosophical question: what is the essence of life? Certainly not foraging for food somewhere on a rubbish pile!

Whatever ideology we might embrace—Christian or communist—all ideologies seek to disclose the human ego, which is one of the principal reasons for man's existence. And this leads us to another question: does humanity have a moral right to give life to many new hundreds of millions of people who are doomed to a wretched existence? Or is it our duty to assure human conditions of life for the already existing billions?

As you know life expectancy is growing. Already now the life-span in Europe has reached seventy-eight years. By the year 2000, it will have grown to eighty-one years. Elderly people will retain their ability to work much longer than now. You are seventy-five years old, Rolf, but even a young person will envy your ability to work. According to statistics for 1987, in the United States people at sixty remain sexually active, if they go in for sport, at the level of thirty-year olds and remain so until they are eighty years of age.

The development of modern society calls for re-evaluation of many established values. Social problems are closely interwoven with ecological ones. For a long time this development was viewed apart from the ecological limitations of our planet Earth. Today the situation is changing rapidly so that we have to take these limitations into consideration. In the past we spoke about the *standard of living*, but now we have to speak about the *quality of life*. How should these problems be solved?

RE   It is true that many people in industrial countries are beginning to understand that the material standard of life is not enough, that the content of life is important so that the time we live on Earth should be meaningful. The problem of size of population is not only of how many people our planet can feed, but how these people live. This is why I am frightened by the forecasts of further urbanization. The content of life is largely determined by how close man is to nature. Besides, the exodus from rural areas exhausts large regions and generates an imbalance in society and even alienation of individuals. This is probably the reason why many industrial enterprises in North America are being moved out of large cities to smaller towns and rural areas.

Or let's take poor countries. When we see the almost beggarly existence of many countries it seems at first glance that everything boils down to the distribution of material wealth. For millions of people even their daily bread is out of reach. And all that at a time when food stocks in the world are big enough to feed all of its population reasonably well.

We must not put up with the fact that, with all our technological achievements, famine still stares in the face of more people than ever before in history. I am convinced that most of the population living in conditions which Marx qualified as degrading to man, will not be satisfied with sops from the wealthy, but will fight for higher material and spiritual standards.

And although formally colonialism has been abolished as a system, the well-off countries (using the current term) continue to pump out of the poor countries the protein, which in the form of ground nuts, beans, soybeans, coconuts, and fish meal is largely fed to livestock, or even to pets. Thus the poor countries go on exhausting their often already depleted soil in order to grow agricultural crops that are favored in the industrially advanced states. A Swedish specialist Georg Borgström calls such agricultural regions ghost areas: we do not see them, although they, directly or indirectly, produce the food for us.

Borgström has also introduced the concept of "the human equivalent." He proceeds from how many people could be fed if they took their nutrients directly from the fruits of the earth and if they did not consume the protein in the tissues of meat cows, pigs and fowl. Upon this assumption the population of the United States would be 1.6 billion human equivalents, and the population of Sweden—95 million.

If we regard as overpopulated a country which cannot feed itself from its own resources, the Borgström formula puts primarily well-off countries in this category.

A Y This model is very impressive. Today about 140 million tons of meat are consumed every year, which breaks down to an annual average of 30 kilograms of meat per capita. We also know that in Nigeria this average meat consumption is 6 kilograms, in China 21 kilograms, in the USSR 62 kilograms, in Britain 75 kilograms and in the United States 110 kilograms. But I quite agree with you that the calculations made on the basis of the human equivalent that you spoke about are much more indicative. These calculations have both sociological and economic aspects. There are 500 million hungry and 40 million starving people in the world. At the same time the countries of Western Europe and the United States have large food surpluses. These surpluses are worth billions of dollars every year. What you just said about where these surpluses come from show that they are mythical surpluses, because they are taken from other countries.

When we see disproportions in the distribution of resources we relate them to distinctions between North and South. Such distinctions are dangerous to the future of mankind not only because they generate potential wars, but also because they bring tremendous pressure to bear upon the natural environment in the developing countries.

It looks as if human society is at the crossroads at a very crucial moment of its existence. The advanced nations must promptly help the developing countries to pass this crucial period which the advanced nations themselves passed centuries ago.

RE I quite agree with you that the well-off nations bear great responsibility for correcting the imbalance in the distribution of products. A tremendous role here is played by our established way of life. Our countries will have to revise the situation drastically.

The truth of the matter is that the world cannot afford to blindly copy the pattern of production and consumption of the well-off countries. It is impossible to extend the material standards of our way of life to all parts of the world precisely because of the tremendous pressure on the resources of the Earth. These resources would not be enough to provide every citizen of our planet with 200 liters of fresh water every day, or with as much meat and electricity as we consume in our own countries. And that aside from such little graces as a new book for one out of every three people every year.

If all the five billion citizens of the Earth, by some technical magic wand, could adopt the pattern of our production and consumption, the wave of affluence would engulf the whole planet . . . However, this wave would very soon ebb away, leaving a plundered planet and our environment a desert.

Distribution of the Earth's resources would be more equitable if the affluent quarter of the population consumed less luxuries—if only because of an instinct of self-preservation—so that the poor countries could get what they simply cannot do without.

AY This is a very acute problem—economically, socially and ecologically.

RE And morally, too!

AY I'm sure that the overwhelming majority of the population in the industrial countries would not consent to having their living standards lowered. The Americans would not like to give up their two cars in every family. And so on. What is the way out? I think we could be helped here by technology, by modern science and economics.

If we analyze the consumption of water in the industrial countries, we shall see that it is decreasing steadily. In the USSR, for
instance, with all its industrial development, the consumption of
water by industry has markedly gone down since 1980. In 1987,
the consumption of water in California dropped by 5 to 10 percent
without seriously affecting the lifestyle of the population of this
most affluent state of the USA. It so happened that the amount of
rainfall was smaller in California that year. The reduction in water
consumption is linked with the economy of water resulting from
the development of waste-free and limited waste technologies. Of
course, this process is not as rapid as we would like to see it.

Our technologists are still very much under the influence of the
pre-ecological way of thinking. They offer us solutions which
simply do not fit in with the general picture of world development.
We must convince our engineers and technologists to be ecologists,
too. The energy crisis which struck the world in the early 1970s
showed that this is not impossible at all. I shall not go into the
causes of that crisis, and shall only point out its principal consequences: a certain reduction of energy consumption in all the advanced countries; the greater attention paid to energy-saving technologies. In North America and Western Europe the amount of
energy has been markedly reduced without prejudice to the national
economies of their countries.

One autumn a few years ago I happened to visit the small town
of York in Britain. To my surprise I noticed that my hotel room
windows did not have double glazing. To keep myself warm I
turned on all the electrical appliances I could find there. Everyone
knows that there are many different ways of building houses, and
that one house keeps warmth in better than another. If houses in
the northern hemisphere were built with better heat insulation, the
countries in this part of the world would save somewhere between
20 and 30 percent of the energy they now consume.

It goes without saying that all our technologies must be orien-
tated toward nature conservation, that they must be more ecologically sound. There are great possibilities here, too. Taken worldwide, half the trips by businessmen between cities and countries

could be unnecessary if people could use more advanced telecommunication facilities than what we do today. Already now people could hold conferences and meetings without actually leaving places where they live and work. Even now they can communicate with one another no matter how far apart they may be. We have already touched upon this problem, and we shall yet talk about it a good deal more. What I have in mind is the production of goods which people can well do without. This means that the advanced countries which consume most of the natural resources must be more ecologically minded than they are today. One thing is clear—the present situation must be changed, no matter what.

RE You have cited a few examples showing why it is necessary to develop resource-saving technologies. All that is well and good. However, such attempts are still very few and far between. Besides they have been ineffectual so far.

We have been talking mostly about distribution between North and South. But if the population continues to grow, even a more equitable distribution will not be able to solve the key problem, the problem of resources.

I would like to touch upon what you said about technology. Very possibly, the modern crisis has been brought about by our sophisticated technical devices in the same measure as by the growth of the population and inequitable distribution.

It is precisely the irrepressible development of technology that has enabled one-quarter of the population of the world to make such a gigantic spurt over the past two centuries. This has liberated most people in the industrial countries of want to an extent they could not even dream about two centuries ago. And yet I often ask myself if present-day technology, the way it is used, has not created more problems than it has solved. Very often our successes are achieved at the expense of the tremendous waste of the limited resources of our planet. Our scheme of production and consumption presupposes appalling squandering of what we extract from nature for our needs. We have got used to it so much that we simply do not notice it any longer.

In the industrial countries, too, many projects disrupt the very foundation of progress just because of the thoughtless treatment of the land, water, forests and the very air that we breathe. Many projects which the advanced countries claim will promote "development," actually render the soil even poorer.

If you follow the trail of a commodity from the source of the raw materials all the way to the rubbish pit, you will see how much waste there is because of faulty technology and the appalling organization of work. When we come to the end of this path we see mountains of waste; the nutrients, water and metals which have served their short-lived usefulness and are then turned into waste and are thrown away instead of being recycled. This means that the very sphere in which we live is gradually turning into a vast rubbish heap.

Let's recall Robinson Crusoe. What happened when he was shipwrecked on a desert island? In our younger days we often put ourselves in Robinson's place and wondered how man's reason and inventiveness enable him to obtain from nature what he needs for his survival. However, this can be worded in a different way: the generous natural environment gave Robinson everything necessary for his survival. While a person is alone, there are no problems: he lives in harmony with the environment. However, if it was not just one Robinson but thousands of them stranded on this island, and if all of them got down to exploiting its natural resources, the island would not have been able to support them. It would have been turned into a barren rock in the ocean.

I think that the multiplicity of forms of man's existence, his requirements, and the technology he uses to exploit the global resources should be correlated with the actual potential of our planet. No invention will ever save us from the need to extract from the natural environment the primary materials for our civilization. In my view we must form a realistic picture of the resources of the planet Earth and on the basis of these findings work out a global economic plan, a kind of worldwide budget in which the expenditures must not exceed the reproductive possibilities of nature.

At the same time we should curb our runaway technical progress and—through all political doctrines and religious concepts—to rally around a clearly defined global objective, something that would call for other, less consuming technologies than those we use today.

A Y   Apropos of the acute question you touched upon earlier—that of redistribution of worldly goods between poor and rich countries— I would like to say again that in spite of the complexity of the development and application of modern technologies, I still think they are the only way to solve the problems of human society. No industrial country would voluntarily abandon the living standards it has achieved. As for modern warfare, it cannot be regarded as an applicable means of equitable distribution of products. In these conditions only an approach to production based on ecological concerns would enable us to build a rational, well-organized world wide economy.

Of course, special responsibility rests with the industrial nations. One cannot demand such ecological measures from the family of an African land-tiller who has to walk miles and miles away to the nearest forest to collect firewood for cooking his meal. But humanity has every right to demand responsible ecological action in all spheres of modern industry. As we said earlier, every person in the world consumes twenty-five tons of mineral raw material, out of which 97 to 98 percent goes to waste. The American ecologist Barry Commoner said thirty years ago that such outstanding achievements of modern civilization as the airplane and the car are the greatest misjudgments and miscalculations of the modern economy with regard to the natural environment. The world is developing according to laws that we do not yet quite understand. For example, growth of consumerism in socialist countries is following close on the heels of the growth of consumerism in the Western world.

As a result of slogans calling for "constantly raising the living standards," the ideology of consumerism in my country has grown to an even greater degree than in some capitalist countries. The only

way out of this situation is to become ecologically conscious in order
to make our production ecologically sensitive at all levels.

Let's do a bit of dreaming. In one of your books you say that it
would be a good idea if we could, with the help of a torch, turn all
materials into their primary components and later recombine them
into new products. In principle, this is waste-free production. With
every passing decade this dream is becoming more and more realistic from a technological point of view. As I think about the future
of humanity, about the happy and prosperous life of our grandchildren, I hope that our technologists will soon translate this dream
into a reality.

RE In the West it is almost heretical to think that the annual growth of
the gross national product is not necessary. Such growth entails the
creation of many artificial needs. The average consumer comes
under a barrage of commercial propaganda that he should part with
what he has to buy something new, to replace commodities that are
quite usable with their equivalents which are different only in that
they have the so-called "new look."

The wasteful technology and the propaganda that call upon us to
be even more profligate with the earth's resources have created a
situation in which, with all our material affluence, we are becoming
poorer and poorer because of the ravaged natural environment. We
are often forced into activities with unpredictable consequences, a
process set off by people who have power but no perspicacity.

I wholeheartedly agree with you that we need an economy and
technology based on ecological factors. We must not treat as waste
the materials that we use briefly in our daily life and then try to get
rid of. It is very important that the human mind, which is much
too often engaged in the humiliating problem of invention of more
and more satanic means of destruction, should engage in the search
for technologies that might harmonize with the implacable "economic laws" of nature.

I call this economic model "the foliage economy." Every autumn,
deciduous trees shed their foliage, which is gradually absorbed by

the soil and is degraded by nutrient-extracting microbes. In the spring these nutrients are returned to the tree and form fresh foliage. This waste-free "foliage economy" sets a pattern that we should do our best to emulate. Otherwise the soil will get poorer and poorer, while we shall literally choke on our own wastes.

A Y   You have spoken about the production of things that we may not need in our daily life. This is something that we here in the USSR are also thinking about. We are producing lots of things we could well do without. Every commodity is meant to have an estimated service life in the interests of the market economy. Designers consider, for example, that a car must serve not more than seven years and must after that be thrown away, and the consumer must spend his money on a new car of a different model. The manufacturers of television sets and tape recorders also build into their products a certain limited service time, which is a clearly anti-ecological approach. This approach is both wrong and immoral, if you like.

In our country eleven billion rubles were spent on the production of containers from 1981 to 1985. This is exactly the amount of money that the state spent on all natural conservation measures, on the protection of water, forests, and air, on the maintenance of national parks, and so forth. A comparable situation obtains in other countries. For example, 5 to 10 percent of the national income is spent on commercial advertising, which is a lot more than on the conservation of the natural environment. This is both anti-ecological and immoral.

R E   Both you and I agree that the overuse of natural resources will lead to their irredeemable destruction. There are quite a lot of examples to illustrate that. In actual fact, all living organisms depend on the thin layer of soil covering the globe. And this thin layer is becoming ever thinner all the time. In our century alone the plunder of the soil has reached tremendous proportions. I have heard that over the past several decades more soil has been destroyed than during the entire history of the human race. According to the United

Nations, in the last quarter of our century the whole of the Earth has a mere 1.2 billion hectares of soil coverage. This figure was presented by the UNEP in Nairobi. But out of this amount, 300 million hectares, notably in overgrazed areas, will vanish by the year 2000 because of erosion. Another 300 million hectares will be absorbed by the growing cities. We have already said that these cities have set off the greatest migration in history. And since the area of cultivated land is limited, we must think of how to go about this problem. Can it be solved at all without first stopping the growth of the population?

A Y I have slightly different figures to bear out this point. It's hard to tell for sure how many millions of hectares will have been lost by the year 2000. Actually this does not matter much whether we shall lose 18 percent or 20 percent of arable land by that time. This is not that important. The other figures I have in mind are nothing short of frightening. Back in 1950 there were 0.24 hectares of arable land per capita in the world. In 1973 this figure shrank to 0.19 hectares, and in 1983 it was a mere 0.15 hectares.

Soil is a remarkable thing. The outstanding Russian scientist Vladimir Vernadsky said that in a sense soil is a living being. The point is that countless numbers of bacteria live in every hectare of soil, and that in addition to microscopic plants and fungi. There are six to seven tons of living organisms in just one hectare of soil 1.5 meters thick. And this living mass enables man to take in a harvest of farm crops, and leave enough in the soil so it can regain its reproducing power. The soil takes 1,000 years to grow a layer just one centimeter thick. It took hundreds of thousands of years in America and the Ukraine to build up a layer of rich, black earth several meters thick. But when the development of farming reached its zenith, the soil began to lose massive quantities of humus, the organic substance it contains. In the United States first, and later in other countries, the loss of humus proceeded at the rate of one centimeter in three years. As a result, farmers in highly agricultural countries have to introduce more and more mineral fertilizers. From the ecological point of view our agriculture is becoming more and more industrialized and depends less and less on the natural recuperative powers of the soil.

There are four principal threats to soil in the world. The first threat is the mechanical destruction coming from wind and water. The second is desertification and aridization when more and more soil becomes unfit for agriculture through desiccation. The third is anthropogenic pollution, or toxification. Strangely enough, toxification is often the result of wrong and inept irrigation. We allow too much water to flow onto the fields. Upon evaporation this water draws salt from layers of earth beneath the topsoil. In some three to five years of intensive irrigation the fields become salinized and we soon lose them. The fourth threat is the direct loss of soil through turning agricultural areas into urban communities, landing fields, and roads.

Already in this century, these four factors have led to rapid reduction in the arable land surface. Now what is the way out? We know that in spite of the reduction of arable land, the output of farm produce in the developed countries is growing through intensification of agriculture. For example, the United States produces so much grain that it can sell it to many countries. Western Europe has the same problem of agricultural surplus of produce. This, of course, entails tremendous expenditure of energy that could eventually prevent modern agriculture from further development. These are the calories that are expended in the fuel for tractors, in the extraction of mineral fertilizers, in the production of pesticides, and so forth.

And yet, speaking of agricultural development, I do not want to sound too pessimistic. New technologies could solve many new problems here, I think. Let me do a bit more dreaming, without losing sight of scientific achievements. In the future we shall be able to even reduce the existing area of arable land. There are projects for creating so-called "enclosed areas" where farm crops will be raised in artificial conditions (referred to here as phytodromes). The effectiveness of such phytodromes is very high. According to calculations, a mere 300 square kilometers of such enclosed areas would be quite sufficient to produce food for the entire population of the USSR. This sounds almost fantastic at first glance, but actually these projects are scientifically tenable. Meanwhile, the continued contraction of the soil area may lead to famine and to growing anthropogenic pressure upon the environment.

RE You have made a very apt reference to the soil as a living being. I think when we speak about our planet we should think of this simile more often. Soil is life. In a sense soil is the primacy of life.

If we follow this line of logic we could very well call the plants that draw their nutrients from the salts and juices of the soil secondary life, and the animals who directly or indirectly feed on plants tertiary life. The life of the plant and animal world depends on the condition of the living soil.

In view of that I, as a nonspecialist, find it difficult to share your faith in the technical solution of the problem of food supply. I have no doubt that we can produce more in the future than we produce today. But in the final analysis all the nutrients are derived from the storehouse of our planet.

You say that as we draw the nutrients from the soil we have to compensate with fertilizers. It is true that what we borrow from the soil we must return to keep up the cycle. But farming has become largely chemicalized, and modern agricultural production may well be compared with a chemical factory. And this, in turn, is fraught with major problems for the life of the soil and for the life of the environment, in general.

Knowing the limited global potential of the soil as the primary source of life, we commit suicide by dissipating it. The corollary here is desertification. You have spoken about the reasons for this phenomenon and said that overgrazing and an excess of fertilizers set off erosion and turn the soil into dust that sweeps over continents and oceans.

A few years ago the UN Food and Agricultural Organization concluded that by the middle of this century we had lost half the soil that once covered our planet. What is worse, by the end of the century half of the remaining soil will have been lost. In the summer of 1987, the UN Committee on Natural Resources submitted a report in which it predicted that one-third of the existing arable land may become a desert. In other words, desert will absorb the lands which today support 950 million people. The figures at my disposal show that in one year alone the desert area increases by six million hectares. All these figures prove that we are heading for self-destruction.

Nevertheless, I think that this problem could be solved. We have satellites that act as a kind of planetary watchmen. They can raise the alarm as soon as they see deserts about to step up their advance. And it is up to the political leaders of the affected countries to decide if they should heed these warnings.

A Y   But this requires money, and not just knowledge and desire.

R E   You are quite right. If soil erosion is particularly intensive in some developing countries, all people are responsible for the preservation of the scant reserves of living soil. These resources should be regarded as belonging to all humanity. As for the advanced industrial nations, they, on top of everything else, should go easy on asphalt for covering land in residential and other areas.

A Y   In addition to that, the problem of desertification is closely linked with widely diverse problems such as agricultural development, poverty, armament, and disarmament. The growing deserts of Africa, notably the Sahelian zone, take up the territory of belligerent countries that just have not got enough resources to turn their attention to these problems. Actually, we know how to fight desertification. Therein lies the difference between this problem and many other problems of environmental protection. However, we cannot interfere for economic and political reasons.

I quite agree that the problem of desertification concerns not only the countries where this is taking place. This is a global problem. And here becoming ecologically conscious seems to be the only way out. This problem closely concerns my country, too. For instance, the drive for breeding more sheep (in Kalmykia, for instance, there are places where the number of sheep grazing there is twenty times as great as the local grasslands can bear) leads to a situation where in three to four years these overgrazed grasslands become a real desert. And after that we shall spend lots of time and money to bring the soil back to its normal condition. The problem of desertification is very important and should by rights be called a global one.

Another crucial problem is the condition of forests, notably the tropical forests. I'd like to stress here that we should focus not on the forests that grow in the temperate zone but on the tropical ones. Perhaps not everybody knows that there is still much forestland in the temperate zone and even in the subarctic. For many decades, about 20 percent of its territory has been taken up by forests. There are even periods when the forest area tends to grow, as was the case in Europe over several decades before acid rains began to fall. Suffice it to say, 32 percent of the territory of Europe is taken up by forest. About 30 percent of the territory of my country is also forest. Of course the forests of the temperate zone have many problems, but they cannot in any way be matched with those of the tropical forests. These forests are the most life-intensive areas of our planet. And this green realm, which is the abode of millions of living species, is shrinking rapidly. The main reasons for it are the utilization of land for agricultural purposes and for the industrial utilization of timber.

If the ravaging of the tropical forests continues at this rate, it will disappear in some fifty to sixty years everywhere except possibly Zaire in Africa and Western Amazonia in South America. And this, in turn, may have a catastrophic effect on the entire living matter of the globe, its biosphere. This raises problems whose solution will not be easy at all.

RE I quite agree with you. The indiscriminate cutting of the rain forests is one of the most serious problems of our time.

The rain forests take up a mere 6 percent of the surface of the globe, but at the same time they harbor as many living species as do all the other ecosystems elsewhere in the world taken together. Many species are truly remarkable for their specialization, and this alone makes the rain forest a regular conglomerate of complex dependencies. Thus the disappearance of one species has a marked effect on many links in this ecosystemic chain.

Wandering about the rain forests I could not help admiring the lush green vegetation, the rich variety of its organisms, and their vitality. It appears that the rain forest can protect itself but in fact it is very vulnerable. This forest is ancient and its soils are depleted and poor in nutrients. In our part of the world most nutrients are contained in the soil. But in the rain forests the main reserves of nutrients are concentrated in the canopy of their trees. The chopping down of forests reduces these green reserves of nature. And when the moment of truth finally comes we shall see that the rain forests, with all their lushness, are nothing but a green desert, which can easily be reduced to an arid desert.

Every second an area of the rain forest equal to the area of a football field disappears. Every year an area of the forest vanishes equal to the size of Austria. Over the past fifteen years an area of rain forest fifteen times as large as Sweden has been wiped out. Reluctance to face the facts has left a trail of destruction on a truly incredible scale.

AY To this I would like to add some facts showing that the industrial countries are just as much interested in preserving the tropical forests. According to the results of some calculations and modeling, the destruction of the forests in Brazil and Zaire will lead to desertification and to a warming up of the climate in the northern hemisphere. In other words, in the near future, this will have a dramatic climatic effect. While it is difficult to make politicians keep this in mind, I think that this fact must at least be remembered by the International Bank for Reconstruction and Development, which in every way encourages tropical forest cutting.

RE What you are saying about the effect of rain forest destruction on the climate of the northern hemisphere has been borne out, for instance, by the U.S. Academy of Science. According to its findings, the blanket destruction of the rain forest bares the soil, which will then reflect the solar heat more intensively. This may affect the entire circulation of the air and may possibly reduce rainfall between the 40° and 85° N. This may badly affect grain production in the temperate zone and consequently the food situation in the world.

I would like to discuss with you, an authority in genetics and evolution, yet another issue. As I understand, no one doubts today that the flora (as well as human beings) of the temperate zone have originated in the tropics. It looks as if the tropics were the workshop of evolution where every new plant and animal species came into being and later migrated to cooler climes and adapted to the new living conditions. Some biologists fear that such paths of migration have been blocked by forest cuttings. And this is what I want to ask you in this connection: do you think that further tree felling in rain forests may affect the continuance of evolution on our small planet?

A Y Yes, I do. This continuance has already been affected. As is known, the tropical forest is home to most of the species living on Earth. So far only 15 percent of these species of the tropical forests have been scientifically described. One discovery is that a large number of species live directly in the canopy of trees. This was established only a few years ago after scientists set up laboratories there. These laboratories are suspended twenty or so meters above the ground, and there researchers live for several weeks and even months. They have discovered an entirely new world.

Some fifteen to twenty years ago scientists thought that there were about 10 million species living in the tropical forests whereas now they put this figure at 30 million. I would like to note here that the tropical forests have some features that make them different from the forests of the temperate zone. For example, the common birch grows in Sweden and in the Soviet Union over millions of square kilometers. By contrast you can see, in just one hectare of tropical forest, several hundred different tree species, each being represented by very few specimens. The cutting of tropical forests leads to a situation in which millions of tree species will be destroyed in the near future. There are no trees that are useless to man. There are tree species whose usefulness has not yet been established. Therefore, even from a purely practical point of view, the cutting of tropical forests—either for wood pulp or for cattle breeding—is madness, evolutionary, ecological, and economic madness. I am convinced that the developed states may find it more profitable to pay large sums of money to the tropical countries for preserving their forests than paying them for wood pulp or meat. This investment will be repaid in fifteen to twenty years.

RE You say that the rich countries should also pay for the preservation of rain forests. This sounds interesting, for this question has been very much on my mind.

You were quite right saying that the rain forest has opened up a new world for us, a new world in the old, familiar world. The most precious thing about the rain forest for all humankind is the tremendous reserves of genes in the great abundance of species, in the material that can play the decisive role in the life of future generations. This reserve can provide us with medicines for yet unknown epidemics and will help us correct our genetic errors, enrich our cereal crops that degenerate because of overcultivation. All citizens of the world must regard the rain forest with its genetic resources as their common property and share responsibility for its fate.

The threat to the rain forest does not come only from the landless peasants who chop down a few trees in order to clear some space for raising crops or for getting firewood, which is becoming scarce in many parts of the world. We can understand and even justify these people and their motives. But we cannot justify the multinationals operating in these forests the way they would never be allowed to do in their own home country. We cannot justify those who ravage Amazonia with fire with no thought about putting the precious timbers to better use, who "conquer" the forest with napalm, driving natives off their land in order to clear vast areas for giant livestock farms. These farms provide meat for those who in the rich industrial countries make big profits from the sale of hamburgers. Oddly enough such grazing lands can be cultivated at a profit for only five to seven years and are afterwards abandoned in favor of new areas.

I think that this whole process must be stopped. The companies operating in the rain forests should abide by a new code of behavior, complete with the universally recognized rules that provide for exercising both caution and respectability. In other words, the companies should sign an obligation to take into account the requirements of the forest itself.

And, finally, a few words about our common responsibility for the preservation of the forest and for the care it needs. I said on a number of occasions that we all must make contributions, and do this not via the impersonal UN fund but by way of personal donations. If we knew that so many pennies from our taxes go for the protection of rain forests, we would be able to better understand in global terms that the question at issue is something for which we bear a common responsibility. It would be wrong to demand that the tropical countries, with their largely overstrained economies, be the only ones responsible for our common future.

AY It is not so easy to find a practical form of payment for the utilization of tropical forests. Such payment would be just as complex as the enactment of a ban on the multinational corporations. But no matter how complex all these questions might be, they must be resolved. If, for example, it turns out that North America breathes the oxygen generated in the tropical forests of South America, this would be good enough reason that this oxygen must be paid for. To resolve the problem of the tropical forests it is very important that more facts should be brought to public knowledge. A lot more must be said about the tropical forests than we do today. Only then would our politicians be able to understand the significance of our arboreal treasure.

RE Denudation of large areas of rain forest wipes out many plant and animal species. However, this happens not only with the tropical forest. We come across this problem all over the world.

Calculations show that early in this century, one species vanished every year. Today we lose one species every day. It is widely believed that by the end of this century one species will vanish from the face of the Earth every minute. Over the last quarter of our century, the planet Earth will have lost one-fifth of the existing plant and animal species.

When people speak about the threat of biospheric extinction, they think in terms of the giant panda and the cheetah, elephant and rhino, the blue whale and the walrus, the white-tailed eagle and the merlin, with many of these animals being on the verge of extinction precisely because of the vain desire to show off hunters' trophies. However, we know nothing at all about most of the vanishing species. They are silently vanishing from the scene not as victims of deliberate killing. Not at all. These species merely bring up the rear of the evolutionary chain because their habitat is exploited by man for the satisfaction of his often very short-term requirements. You noted very aptly that these animals and plants are part of the great global ecosystem where all species exist in close relationship.

Someone once said that we are turning the planet Earth into a sinking ark . . .

A Y I would also like to point out why we are so much concerned about vanishing species. In the process of evolution each species took millions of years to develop. A species is a unique and inimitable combination of genes. The disappearance of any species is an irretrievable loss for the whole world. Our Earth is becoming ever poorer. We are becoming impoverished. Humanity cannot be indifferent to the fact that the number of plant and animal species is shrinking. If we fail to preserve the existing variety of species, future generations of people will find themselves so much the poorer. You, Rolf, summed up the situation very well when you spoke about the silent disappearance of plant and animal species.

I shall cite a few examples illustrating the rapid and widespread disappearance of plant and animal species in Europe. In Sweden 2 percent of all higher plants have vanished and 10 percent are in danger of destruction. In Belgium 5 percent, in some parts of the USSR up to 16 percent of higher plants are threatened with extinction. It is widely believed that about 10 percent of plant species in the world may soon disappear. The same applies to other groups of living organisms. For example, about 40 percent of all mushrooms in West Germany are on the endangered species list. Two-thirds of all butterflies in Europe are threatened with extinction. In West Germany 30 percent of butterfly species have vanished. In Europe 52 percent of freshwater fish species, and more than 60 percent of species of reptiles and amphibians, and 72 percent of bird species may soon vanish; of the 408 bird species a total of 294 species are on the verge of extinction. Half the species of mammals in Europe are also on the endangered species list.

The situation is no better on the other continents. The principal reason for that is the destruction of habitats. However, commercial hunting and fishing continues on a very broad scale. Of great importance here is the dissemination—deliberate or accidental—of new species to new areas. Also widespread is the accidental destruction of animals and plants. To bring all these facts home to every person in the world, I shall cite some examples illustrating the scale of this depredation.

Many of us drive cars. But does the car owner know that if he covers a distance of 10,000 kilometers (which is an average distance for Europe) in just one summer, he kills 1.5 to 1.6 million insects that crash upon his car's windscreen? The number of large animals killed on the roads is also great. In the United States, for instance, 500 million birds, reptiles, and rodents meet their death on the highways. In little Denmark alone more than 6 million frogs, 100,000 hedgehogs and 120,000 hares got killed in just one year in the 1970s. In West Germany about 70,000 roes are killed on the roads. In France more than a quarter of all hares die under the wheels of motor vehicles. This senseless depredation is tragic for the very existence of some species. A great many animals are destroyed by farm machinery; in the Soviet Union more game gets killed under the wheels of tractors and reapers than by shotgun.

There are other examples, too. Oil and gas are extracted all over the world. Moreover casing-head gas is discharged into the air and burned up in flares that become a kind of crematorium for thousands of birds during their migration in the spring and autumn. One October night, about 3,000 birds were burned up over just one such flare in the North Sea. And that only over one flare out of many thousand others burning all over the world. Oil slicks are another source of death for millions of birds.

We have already spoken about a tremendous amount of refuse dumped into the sea. Suffice it to say that 30 percent of sea turtles die because they swallow plastic objects dumped into the water. In the White Sea, for example, we often come upon Greenland seals whose population has over the past several years increased markedly. However, most of these animals look very exhausted. Upon examination their stomachs were found to be cluttered with plastic bags, which account for about 4 percent of deaths among Greenland seals in the White Sea alone.

There are many more such examples that would make the heart of every normal person bleed. I shall cite only a few of them. There are power lines in all countries, which is another cause of death among birds. I think that many people who happened to be near such power lines saw dead birds on the ground as they crashed to their death. When the number of dead birds was counted the statistics thus compiled was shocking. In Kazakhstan, for example, thirty-five steppe eagles die every year along every ten kilometers of power line. When this figure was correlated with the length of all such power lines, the annual death toll was hundreds of thousands of eagles. We knew that birds sometimes get entangled in fishing nets both on lakes and at sea. Nevertheless we were surprised to learn that several million birds die in this way in the North Atlantic alone.

It is a well-known fact that lots of water is pumped out of lakes and rivers to feed the cooling systems of electric power stations. But that in the Soviet Union there are more small fry thus sucked into the cooling systems and then dumped upon dry land than the entire number released by fish farms into lakes and rivers is a shocking fact. The same happens in the United States. There are fourteen thermal and six nuclear power stations on the shores of Lake Michigan. In the water they suck in for cooling, 6 percent of the entire commercially usable fish population in this lake are trapped and killed.

Many birds die of food poisoning. All over Europe today, in places where waterfowl congregate, thousands of pellets or lead shot are found per square meter of ground. The birds often swallow them, and 5 percent of them die from lead poisoning. Today in many states of the United States and in some countries of Europe the use of shot has been banned. When the death of several hundred swans was investigated in Britain over a period of several years, the results showed that 54 percent of the birds had been poisoned by lead sinkers attached to fishing nets. Sometimes I find myself hating my science, because it gives me knowledge that almost makes me weep.

And now about deliberate destruction of birds and animals. In Europe alone, hunters kill, just for sport, more than 16 million waterfowl a year; also 9 million pheasants, grouse, and woodcocks, and as many pigeons and partridges. And what would you say about the destruction the birds of the sparrow family that are to this day caught and killed for food in many countries of the Mediterranean? In Italy, about 500 million songbirds are thus killed every year, and in France about 40 million. Even now in Italy you can order a dish of nightingale hearts. Every year about one million parrots are caught in tropical countries and put in a cage. Six million crocodiles and tens of millions of lizards are hunted on account of their precious leather. Hundreds of millions of frogs are killed for food. And these are merely a few examples of our pressure upon living nature. It does not really matter if this pressure is direct or indirect so long as it despoils the environment.

RE You have given many graphic and grim examples of anthropogenic pressure. These go to prove that man tramples upon his planet both ruthlessly and indiscreetly. The Earth is getting more and more depleted. As you say, our Earth is getting poorer. And this brings us to another problem—the water resources of our planet. The

Earth is the only known planet that has water which is the cradle of life and its sine qua non.

The number of thirsty mouths is growing. At the same time water consumption in industry and agriculture is increasing. Our factories and plants are even thirstier than we are here. In many places pressure upon water resources is greater than the ability of nature to renew them.

Ironically, the only "water" planet in the solar system is becoming a thirsty planet. Actually water does not disappear but circulates between the seas and oceans and the clouds, from the clouds it drops down in the form of rain which gives rise to flowing water. Ninety-seven percent of the world water resources is concentrated in the seas and oceans, and only 3 percent comes in the form of fresh water with 75 percent of this amount tied up in glaciers and the polar ice caps. Thus the continents account for less than 1 percent of the world water reserves, most of it groundwater. We often refer to Lake Baikal as an inland sea and speak with admiration about the mighty Amazon. However, lakes and rivers contain only thousandths the amount of the world water reserves.

And it is these thousandths that our life depends on, which calls for our wise and rational treatment of this precious wealth. Moreover, these fresh-water resources are distributed about our planet very unevenly. Many poor countries suffer from a chronic water shortage. Most women on our planet tote water in clay pitchers and hollowed-out pumpkins, carrying one child in their arms and another in their womb. These unborn babies also need water. How much physical effort would these women be spared should the sources of water be closer to their home! Technically, it would be quite possible to supply all families with water drawn somewhere nearby. But as we found out already on the first day of our dialogue, the world prefers to spend money on missiles and squander it in other ways.

A Y The problem of water is a global problem. As any other global problem it has social, political, and environmental aspects.

One ton of fresh water in the developed countries costs ten cents.

This is good, specially purified drinking water. By contrast, one ton of fresh water in the countries of the Third World costs twenty dollars. This water is of poor quality, unpurified and heavily infected with bacteria. Two hundred times as expensive! This is not only a difference in natural conditions. It is also the difference between the social and political conditions.

We know that a person needs 15 liters of water a day for a more or less decent existence. In the developed countries the average per capita consumption of water is 100 liters a day. This is the minimum for modern civilized consumption. In the majority of developed countries the daily per capita consumption of water in urban areas is 500 liters. Of course it would take great efforts to provide the whole world with this much water. However, society would have to solve this problem at all costs. Some comfort here can be derived from the fact that water is a renewable resource, as you say. If we channel a sufficient amount of money and resources into the improvement of our water economy, say the money saved from a reduction in armament spending, we would be able to provide the whole world with fresh water. However, there is still a long way to go to achieve this goal.

I shall give you just one example. Moscow is one of the biggest cities in the world. It is still growing and it needs more and more water. About forty years ago a special canal was built to draw water from the Volga. Now, in the 1980s, we have realized that this water is not enough. Engineers and building planners, who still think in traditional ways, thought another canal should be built, starting from yet another storage lake in the upper reaches of the Volga.

RE I wonder what is going to happen to the Volga.

AY And this is precisely what scientists want to hear from our politicians. There was a heated discussion in the press, with many arguments for and against. The final decision was "no" to both the new canal and any new dam. This discussion revealed that 25 to 30 percent of the water is dissipated through leaking taps, disintegrating underground pipelines, and so forth. It would be a lot better for our water supply if we could make better use of the existing facilities, and thus save a lot of water, the amount of which would be as great as that supplied by the projected canal. It is true, though, that technically this is not easy at all, for hundreds of kilometers of underground pipelines would have to be checked.

RE This has put me in mind of another project that has been widely discussed in the Soviet Union. I mean the plan of changing the course of some northern rivers flowing into the Arctic Ocean. The idea was to divert them to the south in order to irrigate vast agricultural areas. This project was opposed by many, including my friend Valentin Rasputin, who as a writer embodies the conscience of the people in the struggle for the protection of the environment in the Soviet Union. This project, just like the plans for a new canal from the Volga to Moscow which you spoke about, illustrates how technocrats completely ignore ecological realities.

What would happen if the mighty rivers carrying fresh water to the Arctic Ocean were diverted from their present course? Could it be that the ocean would then become colder, and its ice would move farther to the south? In other words, would this result in some dramatic changes in the climate, which means that the whole project would then concern not only the Soviet Union, but also its neighbors—Finland, Sweden and Norway. Do such projects not raise the question that, on the one hand, we should not ignore ecological laws and, on the other, that it is necessary, upon starting any new major project in one country, to reckon with its possible consequences for others?

You have spoken about water leakage in old worn-out water pipes. What would you say to the way factories waste water using obsolete technologies, which oddly enough are still regarded as modern? The various articles used in our daily life require tremendous expenditure of water for their production. Also much water goes for cooking, for washing and for cooling. For instance, the production of one ton of paper requires 100 tons of water. The manufacture of one car requires 250 tons of water, let alone the production of plastics. A thermal power station consumes 600 tons of water per ton of coal burned, whereas nuclear power stations consume whole rivers. We cannot any longer afford such wasteful luxury.

You spoke about reduction in the consumption of water in some areas. This is a good sign. Meanwhile, a few years ago some western specialists reckoned that by the end of this century water requirements in industry would be ten times what they are now. This means that it is necessary to develop new less water-intensive technologies as soon as possible. Why should not regions with relatively rich water resources export fresh water to countries suffering from drought and thirst, and do that via pipelines as with oil and gas? Why should our industrial enterprises not make repeated use of fresh water in the so-called closed systems?

Of special significance is the utilization of groundwater for local irrigation in many regions of the world. Groundwater accumulates very slowly. I would say that there are fresh water reservoirs deep underground that can trace their origin back in the Bronze Age, possibly even earlier when the climatic conditions were different. And when we draw large amounts of water from their subterranean reservoirs, the process is comparable to major mining processes. In many places, as in some areas in India, the extraction of water exceeds its accumulation.

To my mind, our discussion about the reserves of fresh water in the world will inevitably lead us to believe that the future of the world community will largely depend on whether we shall learn to treat water as nature's wonderful creation, the source of life for the present and future generations.

A Y I realize that the problem of water is your special interest. You even wrote a book called *The Drops of Water—the Drops of Time*. I would like to add here that man must take a new, different attitude to fresh water. Indeed, water is a unique natural resource, but man has not yet rejected his old, extravagant approach to the utilization of water. We have much too long been used to the idea that we can only take and take. . . . As a result, underground water reservoirs are expended faster than they are replenished. This is true. Another major problem is pollution of these reservoirs with pesticides and fertilizers. The easily soluble pesticides penetrate water reservoirs with particular ease. This is yet another example of how difficult it is to forecast the ecological consequences of technological progress. In 1985 alone, 80 percent of the water wells in Florida had to be shut down because of the dangerously high level of pollution with pesticides. There are other sources of pollution, however. I read somewhere that in a small West German town a faucet spouted oil instead of water. As it turned out, a few years before a railway train loaded with oil had overturned several miles away.

It is bad to have too little water, but too much water may also be bad. Uncontrolled irrigation leads to the loss of vast land areas through salinization. I know about some African zoologists who have studied the effect that rising groundwater has on nature preserves. They write that fresh water springs attract so many animals that they literally trample out everything around, turning the once rich fertile land into a desert.

RE I know about it, and I even have examples of this at firsthand.

AY You are quite right saying that the one-sided treatment of water problems in one part of our planet may affect areas hundreds and even thousands of kilometers away. In our country one such painful problem is that of the Aral Sea. This is an inland sea in Kazakhstan that used to be fed by the two largest rivers in Soviet Central Asia— the Amu-Darya and Syr-Darya. Today the water of these rivers has been used up for irrigation purposes. As a result, the surface area of the Aral Sea is now half of what it once was and continues to shrink.

Moreover, the wind that disseminates salt from the bottom of the sea has an adverse effect on areas hundreds of kilometers away. Besides, there is less rainfall hundreds and even thousands of kilometers from this sea. It may well happen that the disappearance of the Aral Sea will affect the climate of the whole of Central Asia.

RE Looks like we have touched upon all the principal global problems of the environment. Maybe we should get down to problems that concern man more directly?

A Y Before we pass on to problems that have a direct effect on man, I
would like briefly to recall some of the major problems of almost
global import. I can cite several such problems.

A considerable part of our planet is covered with the tundra and
arctic deserts both of which are very fragile ecosystems. Suffice it to
say that even a slight incautious intrusion may have a very lasting
effect. Here is an example. A tractor or a cross-country vehicle may
leave a trail that does not heal for thirty to forty years. According
to our assessments, 65 to 67 percent of the tundra has been affected
by anthropogenic activities.

Another major problem is the shrinking of the traditional landscapes in prairies, steppes, and savannas. The steppes and prairies
were the first known landscapes that man used for agricultural purposes. Today only small parts of the steppes and prairies have sur-
vived, and mostly in nature preserves. People must retain at all
costs what has been left of the prairies, steppes, and savannas in
order to use them as models for nature restoration work in the future.

R E Is this possible?

A Y It is still possible. Possible because the plant species of the steppes
can survive in the remaining few nature preserves, small as they are.
Significantly, the biological productivity of the steppes and prairies
is much higher than even that of forests. These are not our fields
sown to one farm crop. Hundreds, and even thousands, of species
once grew in one place. They absorbed solar heat and easily repro-
duced themselves. In the future our fields must also be used for
raising several crops, not just one. And that is why we have to know
more about the life of steppes and prairies.

R E This, of course, applies to the savanna, too.

A Y There is still another global problem. This is the wetlands in coastal
areas and river estuaries. Also mangroves. Two-thirds of commercial
varieties of fish are linked in their life cycle with this narrow strip

of coast. Vaddensee, Kamarg, also the Scandinavian fjords are wetlands that are vanishing at catastrophic speed. Over the past century about 50 percent of the wetlands have been either taken up with construction sites or ruined by dumping rubbish, which has led to irreversible environmental changes. This is also a major problem not to be ignored.

DAY

4

THE ESSENCE OF THE PROBLEM IS SIMPLE AND
CAN BE SUMMED UP IN JUST ONE QUESTION: HOW
CAN I, A PERSON ENTITLED TO A DECENT LIFE,
PUT UP WITH THE FACT THAT SOME INDIVIDUAL
OR SOME FACTORY OR SOME CONCERN POLLUTES
THE AIR I BREATHE, THE WATER THAT WILL GO
INTO MY BLOODSTREAM OR INTO THE MINIATURE
OCEANS OF MY CELLS, INTO THE SOIL WHOSE
SALTS OR JUICES WILL FEED ME?

—ROLF EDBERG

WHAT CAN ONE PERSON DO IN THE FACE OF THE
POORLY MANAGED ECONOMIC SET-UP OF THE
HUMAN RACE? HE STANDS UP AGAINST ORGANIZED
INDUSTRY AND COMPLEX ECONOMIC
AND POLITICAL SYSTEMS.

—ALEXEI YABLOKOV

■

RE At the end of our talk yesterday you touched upon the pollution and poisoning of our water reservoirs, which raises an important question: how do we treat our natural environment?

Ecology does not distinguish between different political systems. There is no such political system that would, of its own, ensure a good and healthy environment. Capitalism with its rivalry and its profit chasing, the Soviet system with its centralization and bumbling bureaucracy . . . Neither system has coped with the ecological crisis of industrial society so far.

Here we are closely linked one with the other, because environmental pollution knows no boundaries. We in the West shall not be able to solve our problems without the same problems being solved in Eastern Europe. On its part Eastern Europe will not be able to solve its problems separately from Western Europe. Regardless of political doctrines and ideological convictions we coexist in Europe's biosphere.

Taken in a broader sense, we live in a biosphere whose right name is Tellus. Winds have no passports. They ignore our customs offices and easily transport pollutants and toxic substances across all borders, and make all of us citizens of the World Polluted States.

Someone once said: one of the strangest features of the war that man is waging against nature is that nobody has declared this war. We are not fully aware that we are fighting this war. Until recently many of our destructive actions were committed unconsciously, not deliberately. The smokestacks of our factories were belching progress. We did not see the harmful substances hiding deep in the smoke. Water got gradually saturated with industrial and domestic wastes, and because we did not see them we thought that they disappeared of themselves. However, nothing disappears. Everything comes back, albeit in other combinations that are often even more poisonous than those that entered water in the first place.

Both industrialists and technologists contended that they were transforming nature for the good of man. They sincerely believed that their intentions were good.

Now we've grown wiser. Although we still do not know many things, we have enough knowledge to see that nature must be treated more carefully than it has been up to now. Ignorance can no longer be used as an excuse. Today the destruction of the vital elements of the environment is often the result of outright cynicism coupled with indifference that is probably equally dangerous to nature.

A Y We shall discuss problems that are of equal significance to socialist and capitalist countries. It is true that our two systems are in competition with one another. At the same time our two systems are getting increasingly dependent on each other, this dependence stemming from the common nature of our planet. We, that is, capitalist and socialist countries, shall either accommodate our relations with the natural environment, shall learn how to live in peace with it, or shall perish—all of us together. Ronald Reagan once said that if the planet Earth were attacked by visitors from outer space, Americans would soon make friends with the Soviet Union. We need no such visitors from outer space. The conditions of the natural environment are such that we must pool our efforts right now to save the Earth.

None of the countries can actually pull out of the global ecological game. The Swedes might want to shut themselves off from European ecological problems. However, the 200 kilograms of sulfur that yearly descend upon every citizen of Sweden mostly come, or rather fly in, from abroad. The same could be said about my own country. The tremendous amounts of pollutants are brought in from other countries, and vice versa.

I shall cite an example which is close to me by reason of my profession. Together with my Swedish colleagues I study Baltic seals, which are in an appalling state of health. Their population is shrinking rapidly, because, being at the top of the food chain, they accumulate pollutants in their body. Many of them either stop procreating, or just die. To find out what is actually happening to the Baltic seals, it was important to see how they live in a reservoir filled with absolutely clean water. So we decided that Lake Baikal which, incidentally, is populated by seals of a species close to that in the Baltic, was precisely this ecologically ideal reservoir. However, when we studied the chemical composition of the fat of Baikal seals we spotted the presence of DDT! Surprisingly, this chemical had never been used either in Baikal or anywhere around it. As it turned out, the DDT that had accumulated in Baikal seals had been brought here from Africa and Southern Asia!

You are quite right in saying that ecological problems face both capitalist and socialist countries equally. Both you and we have to look for an optimal solution to the same ecological problems. Some twenty-five years ago I visited India as a member of a zoological expedition. In those days Madras was in the grip of hot political debates about who would head the local municipal council—the Left or the Right. But the Mayor of Madras remarked: "Whoever takes my place will have to come to grips with the same old problems of water supply, rubbish disposal, and disease." In a socialist society there is no private ownership of natural resources. But incompetence, inertia, and mismanagement lead to no less serious ecological consequences than the way the capitalist monopolies of the West work.

Thus ecologically we are coming to what is known as the new political thinking, or the understanding of the need for unity of mankind in the face of common global problems.

RE Yes, wherever people might live they are up against the same problems. Landscapes may look different, but the environment is indivisible.

Speaking of pollution and poisoning, we must always regard man as part of the environment. When I drink a glass of water in the morning, I irrigate my tissues with the moisture that came here from the proto-ocean and then went through numerous transformations. This water may once have been rivers, clouds, and rains. It may have hung in the form of early morning mist over Lake Baikal, and then risen high in the air when it was exhaled by myriads of living creatures. Then it may also have been used for cooling a nuclear reactor. The air that goes through the tissues of my body today may have passed through luxuriant coniferous branches or the foliage of the rain forest. It was once inhaled by Buddha and Genghis Khan. It also got mixed up with factory smoke and was forced through the exhaust pipes of numerous cars. And since both the water and the air, in their continuous circulation, pass through our bodies, by using the water and the air we ourselves have also polluted our own tissues. Similarly, our muscles and internal organs are made up of the humus that connects both former and future life.

It seems to me we must always remember that we are part of such processes. As we sum up our actions we can well operate within technical and political categories, although, if we get right down to it, the main problem is that of morals.

A Y You are right saying that we are part of the circulation of matter. But, unfortunately, each one of us as a single person cannot take this circulation in at a glance. Incidentally, the old Greeks spoke almost in the same words as you about the unity of the world. Omar Khayyam and Avicenna said that, too. But that was simply a remarkable prevision, and not scientific knowledge. Today we are equipped with such knowledge. However, this knowledge has not yet been transformed into the logic of human behavior. We tend to forget that we are a tiny particle of this circulation, and that we also disrupt this circulation. To put it bluntly, we are chopping off the branch on which we sit.

It has been proven scientifically that global problems will have an ever greater effect on our material culture, on every person, and on humankind as a whole. And it seems to me that humankind as a whole does not yet fully comprehend all the negative aspects of what so-called scientific and technological progress brings to society. We are not yet ready to understand the negative effects of this progress. One reason for this is the inertial processes in the biosphere. They are different in scale and proportion from the processes in our consciousness. Several decades may pass before a drop of Baikal mist reaches the waterfalls of Africa and then cools the atomic power stations on the Baltic or on Lake Michigan. But as we live today, we have to solve our problems without delay—tonight, or tomorrow morning. Everyone of us thinks that the air he breathes is what it was yesterday or a year ago. And he thinks so in spite of the fact that, according to scientific tests, the state of the atmosphere changes every year.

The question suggests itself: what can be done to turn the largely well-known ecological laws into moral imperatives? I would like to recall the four aphoristically worded laws of ecology: "Everything is linked with everything else," "Everything must go somewhere," "Nature knows better," "Nothing can come out of nothing." How can these ecological laws be translated into our daily political and economic life? This is the problem.

When an electric power station is still under construction, its economic effect is calculated for a period of fifteen to twenty years. I do not think this is the right approach. The economic effect must be calculated at least over a period of three generations of people, because by doing so we bear responsibility for the quality of life of my grandchildren. The older generation must be responsible for all the younger generations that exist with it simultaneously.

RE You ask how a person who is beset with routine economic and political problems can actually feel that he is part of one great and indivisible ecological whole? This is a very important and far from simple question.

It is necessary to make each of us aware of what we will be confronted with if we do not stop despoiling the environment, considering the terrible consequences this profligacy will have for future generations.

Some of the toxins that enter the organism of a mother-to-be will reach the ovaries and the fetus, because a pregnant woman and fetus have common blood circulation. The most terrible thing about all this is the fact that these toxins are not confined to the body of a person who got them from without, but will be passed on to the baby. What is more, the newborn baby will get more toxins through his mother's milk than he received in his mother's womb over the nine months of gestation.

Like many other living creatures, we feel strongly attached biologically to those we give life to. We should appeal to this feeling in our fellow human beings and in this way explain the risk that our children and grandchildren are exposed to. Therein lies the key role played by scientists, writers, and, especially, schoolteachers. Such information must be part of the elementary knowledge taught at all schools.

If ordinary people come to understand how the exhaust fumes from cars, industrial effluence, and other wastes affect their health, also the health of their children and grandchildren, they will be prepared to increase the pressure on those who make ecologically harmful decisions. Such pressure is mounting, but apparently it is yet not strong enough. It should be increased many times over.

AY From the ecological point of view the world is very contradictory, and the decisions made in this respect are in no wise simple. You have put it very aptly that the fetus in a mother's womb is poisoned by the same toxic substances as have poisoned the mother. But there is still another crying contradiction here. A child gets born, and it must be nursed. In the industrial countries artificial nursing was very popular. However, it became a known fact a few years ago that artificially nursed children are not as physically strong and healthy in their adulthood and later years as those who were breast-fed. They are susceptible to more diseases. They suffer from alimentary malfunctions all their life, and their nervous system on the average is more affected. It looks as if artificial nursing should be given up in favor of breast-feeding. That was a common belief. However, today, with the global pollution of the environment, every nursing mother passes on to her child DDT, PCB (polychlorinated biphenyls) and many other substances that can badly affect the health of her child as compared to formula-fed children. It has turned out that the formula and other baby foods often contain smaller amounts of toxins than does mother's milk!

This is the complex reality of our modern world!

RE I agree that all this is very complicated. There is no such thing as easy solutions. Actually, the essence of the problem is simple and it can be summed up in just one question: How can I, a person entitled to a decent life, put up with the fact that some individual, or some factory or factories pollute the air I breathe, the water that will go into my bloodstream or into the miniature oceans of my cells, into the soil whose salts and juices will feed me!

This very question must sound like a clarion call for a revolt, a revolt across all the political and ideological boundaries against those who poison the environment.

AY But what can one person do in the face of the poorly managed economic set-up of the human race? In the face of organized industry and complex economic and political systems? I think that in these conditions education and the dissemination of ecological knowledge must follow on the heels of the struggle against direct environmental pollution. Everything that proves to be anti-ecological must be declared immoral. Only in this way will politicians and decision makers follow the implacable logic of ecology.

RE One of the reasons why this problem sounds so complicated is the question that we often ask ourselves: what should rightly be called poison?

Strictly speaking, there are no simple substances which are poisonous per se. There are dangerous concentrations and combinations of different substances. Some of them are not only harmless, but even useful when taken in small doses, although the same substances become lethal when their dosage is increased.

We found out belatedly that some chemicals, if dumped upon the natural environment, may have very undesirable consequences. Some time ago, in fact until fairly recently, DDT was spoken of in glowing terms, that "never before in the history of entomology was there a substance that was so effective in ridding man of harmful insects." Today we take a different view of DDT. We have a lot of examples of how even the most innocuous substances become, under the influence of different natural factors, destructive for both animals and plants.

We produce lots of different substances that until recently did not exist in the environment. According to the United States Academy of Sciences, we have 70,000 chemical preparations in use. These are synthetic substances that do not occur in nature. Out of this number, four hundred have been found in the human organism. Some of them have a toxic effect at the very start. Most of them have never been tested, and their action on human organs is unknown. We do not know how far nature's biodegrading powers can go. It looks as if no one has a clear idea about the stuff that enters the market in ever greater amounts. This is a very worrisome circumstance, for any mistake can have a lasting and far-reaching effect.

Production of toxins takes its ultimate form in combat gases that have been stockpiled in the military arsenals of many countries, not just the great powers. So far their application has been held back by the well-founded apprehension that a mere change in the direction of the wind could drive the gas against those who released it in the first place. Now a tricky method has been invented to avoid such a risk. An artillery shell is filled with isolated substances, each one being completely harmless if taken separately from the other. When the shell explodes upon impact these substances get mixed up, forming a highly toxic gas that poisons everything within active range.

In the same way what we dump into the natural environment can have consequences that we cannot always foresee. This is to say that we have to be extremely cautious about what we do not yet know, and particularly about what we do know.

A Y So it turns out that a pollutant, or a toxin, is practically any substance that emerges where it is not supposed to be, and not at the time when it is expected to be, and not in amounts in which it should be. Here is a good example. For thousands of years manure from livestock has been a boon for the farmer, because it guarantees a new crop. But man has set up giant farms, placed thousands of animals side by side. As a result, the tremendous amount of dung has become a major pollution problem. Man creates thousands of new substances every year. They are different from what nature creates and are therefore dangerous to it. Actually, these new substances are dangerous in any amount. Even ceramics and glass are dangerous, also the neutral plastic that we spoke about earlier on, the plastic that causes the death of turtles and seals. To sum up, we can say that all new substances that are strangers to nature, substances that have been made by man, are dangerous. Therefore, they are all potential pollutants.

Today we shall speak about agricultural pollution. This is one of the most important problems humankind faces today. Since 1980, the United Nations has regarded the threat to living nature coming from farming as one of the four burning issues. I shall dwell on it in more detail. Agriculture provides us with food and is at the same time very dangerous. There are two major problems that affect the life of man and that of the natural environment in the sphere of agricultural production. The first such problem is the growing application of pesticides, and the second is the use of mineral fertilizers.

It is all clear when it comes to fertilizers. All I want to add is a remark about the nitrates. Over the past several years, the inordinate application of nitric fertilizers in my country has boosted harvests, has made watermelons larger, vegetables cleaner and more attractive. But, understandably, people are no longer eager to buy all this good-looking produce, mainly because the large amounts of nitrates in fruit and vegetables cause mild food poisoning. But what is still more dangerous is the fact that the nitrates are transformed in our bodies into so-called nitrosamines, and these, in turn, can touch off malignancy. The juicy, large, and attractive products have sharply increased the risk of this terrible malady, which sums up our anti-ecological approach to life itself.

RE Before passing on to pesticides I would like to say a few words about overfertilization. We have some bitter experience on this score in Sweden: overfertilized fields give up nitrogen to ground and running water that eventually drains into the sea where it is ingested by planktonic algae, called peridinea, which absorb so much oxygen that crayfish and other bottom creatures die, whereas fish either perish or are forced to leave their habitat. This picture can be seen along the entire sea coast in western Europe. I am sure that the coastal areas of the Soviet Union have the same problem. In Sweden the government and parliament have decreed a reduction by half the amount of nitrogen fertilizers introduced into the soil. It seems, however, that this reduction is not sufficient.

Sweden and another four European countries proposed signing an international agreement on a 30 percent reduction in the discharge of nitric oxides. Other nations opposed this move. After that the said five nations attempted to reach an agreement on freezing the amount of discharge at the level it was as of 1987. But this move, too, was rejected by representatives of the East European countries, the United States, Britain, and Italy.

This is just a prelude to our discussion of pesticides, which is a world-wide problem.

AY What you have said brings me back to the subject of fertilizers. You've touched upon a very important aspect of their application. It is widely believed that somewhere between half and three-quarters of the fertilizers that are used in the fields are washed out of the soil and carried into rivers, lakes, and seas. One must not forget that the vegetables and other products saturated with fertilizers do not keep well. I would like to recall that water reservoirs have an overdose not only of fertilizers, but also domestic detergents. The peridinea and other microalgae propagate rapidly, which is true. However, this is not the only factor affecting aquatic life. Sometimes various toxic substances appear in these conditions, making the use of fish for food highly dangerous.

Now a few words about pesticides. To understand the magnitude of the problem, I would like to cite just one figure. Altogether, some 20 to 25 billion dollars worth of pesticides are sold throughout the world every year. This means that on the average about 400 to 500 grams of pesticides are used per person annually throughout the world. In the United States and the USSR this figure rises to 2 kilograms. In areas of intensive farming, up to 50 kilograms of pesticides are used per person. Careful analyses have shown that not more than 3 percent (usually less than 1 percent) of the pesticides "hit the target," the rest being carried out from the fields into the air, water, and soil.

Thus the pesticides are a kind of pollutant that is deliberately introduced into the environment. I would like to recall that at first the pesticides were used to kill pests, and that initially agriculture benefited from them. They are a powerful chemical weapon that effectively destroy many forms of life. With the years, however, it became clear that the pesticides were not as effective as they seemed at first. Moreover, the pesticides are very dangerous because they affect all living things. In spite of the fact that over the past several decades a switch has been made from the very dangerous and stable organochlorides of the DDT type to the rapidly biodegradable phosphorous-organic carbamates and pyrethrins, all pesticides are, nevertheless, ecologically dangerous.

What is more, the effect from using pesticides is getting progressively smaller. In the 1940s, 7 percent of the farm crops in the United States were destroyed by pests, whereas in the 1980s this figure has risen to 13 percent. Significantly, the amount of pesticides used in the United States over the same period has risen ten times over!

RE You spoke about harmful insects. But would it be correct to call any insects harmful? If one insect population or another becomes too large it truly can inflict great harm upon animals and plants. However, don't we ourselves speed up the growth of certain populations by making our farming too one-sided?

This situation brings forth a new chain that is alien to nature: monocultures stimulate the development of certain types of insects. When this happens we hurriedly begin to spray our fields. Maybe we have already made a mistake at the beginning of the chain, as well as at the end of it?

A Y This is exactly what most scientists think. The appearance of pests in the fields clearly shows that our methods of farming are faulty. There are no such thing as pests in nature. It is man who creates them. The question is how to manage our agriculture correctly in order to avoid pests. Actually, we know the answer. I can say, for example, that we should move away from monocultures to multi-crop systems, that we should sow several crops in our fields, and not just one crop. There are also other methods of farming that will help us avoid pest propagation. However, in reality today we are still producing millions of tons of pesticides. It looks as if this chemical invasion will continue for another decade. This is why we have to speak about the dangers posed by pesticides, something that many people do not know. They do not know of these dangers, not only because of the lack of scientific information, but very often because this information is not brought home to the public, and very often deliberately, it seems.

For instance, it is a well-known fact that pesticides, like any other toxic substance, become dangerous when they reach a certain concentration. However, very few people know that the action of pesticides is cumulative and increases with time. In other words, pesticides, like radiation, are chronoconcentrative toxins. This means, in turn, that concentration limits come in two forms: a permissible one-time concentration and a permissible diurnal concentration.

Pesticides also destroy vast numbers of animals for which they are not meant at all. According to statistics, in many areas of our country, of the total number of elks, wild boars, and hares destroyed for one reason or another, 80 percent die of agricultural pollution. Thirty percent of the fish that die perish from agricultural effluence. Even in low concentrations the pesticides can induce behavioral changes in animals. For example, a pesticide called sevin, even in an infinitesimal concentration of one-billionth, can change the behavior of large schools of fish: their movement becomes uncoordinated. This toxic concentration creates a chemical background in our biosphere. It looks as if the behavior of all living creatures has been somewhat changed by the presence of pesticides.

RE I want to ask you a question as a geneticist. Is there any risk of pesticide contamination directly affecting our genes? As far as I understand, this question has not yet been cleared up conclusively, so we cannot expect to have an exhaustive reply to it. Nevertheless, it seems to me that examinations carried out on other living species, and partly on our own, enable scientists to draw well-founded conclusions.

AY Unfortunately, the results of such examinations are not at all encouraging. Pesticides hold second place among all other substances that provoke mutations. It is difficult to tell how many mutations have actually taken place, for no such experiments can be made on man. So other objects have been selected for experimentation: microorganisms, blood cells, mice, and plants. One test shows the ability to change DNA only in 40 percent of the pesticides under study. Two tests show 75 percent of the pesticides being mutagenic. For four tests the figure is 94 percent and, finally, seven tests show that all 100 percent of the analyzed pesticides are mutagenic. Special calculations show the extent of danger to humanity. About 2 percent of newborn babies have congenital diseases. You may say that 2 percent is not much, but if you think that these 2 percent stand for millions of people and that these genetic changes are retained in the actual population, that they get combined and recombined, forming what we call the genetic load, then you realize the magnitude of the problem.

The pesticides not only cause genetic changes, they also upset the normal course of pregnancy and increase the number of stillborn babies and spontaneous abortions. Children born in regions with intensive use of pesticides are marked for their poor and slow physical development. Some people believe that industrialized farming is among the most hazardous occupations. Altogether, tens of thousands of people become poisoned with pesticides every year, and several million people are in danger of severe poisoning.

I have spoken about the catastrophic consequences of the application of pesticides for human health. Actually pesticides affect all living things. They can, for instance, upset the synchronism of animal propagation: males and females may be ready for fertilization at different times. An example of this is frogs in the North Caucasus. Both males and females are healthy and are ready for propagation, but because the periods of their sexual activity occur at different times no fertilization is possible. I give this example just to show once more that pesticides can have a destructive effect on living nature. The wide range of side effects of pesticides very often leads to consequences other than those that people want to achieve by using them. For example, a campaign was mounted in the Republic of Côte-d'Ivoire against the tsetse fly. The main agent used was deltametrine, a newly developed pesticide. This toxin is so potent that it should be used in very tiny doses—a mere 12.5 grams per hectare. But after the dispersal of this deadly agent the tsetse fly continued to live practically undisturbed, whereas eleven endemic varieties of fish out of the fifty-five had vanished.

RE   I would like to cite another example from Africa. For ten or so years now a grandiose project has been underway south of the Sahara, planned over a period until the year 2010. On the territory of seven million square kilometers efforts have mounted to destroy the tsetse fly and clear the way for livestock breeding. This area, equal to the territory of the United States, is being treated with mountains of pesticides: DDT and dieldrin, the use of which has been banned in Europe and the United States. Also endosulfan of which even its manufacturers say that it must not be used near water reservoirs and swamps.

Many environmentalists doubt that this project is reasonable. They fear that these areas will eventually be overgrazed and depleted. I would like to emphasize here that the problem involves the use of marginal zones that can support livestock for five years, and not more, after which the exposed humus will be destroyed by wind erosion. Maybe it would be better to obtain protein by regularized shooting off of antelopes and other animals that have adapted themselves to the local conditions over the long period of evolution?

I have quoted this example only because you mentioned the tsetse fly in your apocalyptic survey.

A Y This is a very convincing example of the anti-ecological approach to problems. Every year the number of vermin and the insects that we fight with chemicals is growing, and so is their resistance to pesticides. For the first time such resistance was noted in citrus-eating insects called the San Jose scale in California in 1913. In 1983 there were 434 insect species and other invertebrates insensitive to pesticides. Among them were the common housefly, the cockroach, and so forth. In some ten to fifteen generations of intensive use of pesticides, any suppressed species with a sufficiently massive population builds up resistance. This is almost a rule. The tsetse fly cannot be coped with by means of chemicals.

When we speak about pesticides we have in mind insecticides, herbicides, fungicides, and so forth. In this connection I would like to say a few words about herbicides. It is true that very effective herbicides have been developed to destroy weeds. We spray green shoots, leaving only rye and barley and destroying the remaining plants. But as it happens the use of herbicides leads to intensive soil erosion and to the loss of topsoil. This, in turn, requires the use of additional doses of chemical fertilizers. What a vicious, senseless, anti-ecological cycle!

R E I have already asked if it is correct to refer to insects as harmful when we actually have in mind their different varieties. What we call weeds may well be noncultivated plants that also play a part if viewed broadly. What would you say about that?

A Y The use of the word "weed" is very relative, of course. This is what grows not where we think it should. After a long struggle against so-called weeds many of them eventually have to be protected in Europe so that they will not disappear as species altogether.

But let's go back to the use of chemicals. With time the place of the species destroyed by chemicals is taken over by other species of unwanted wild plants. As a result their number will grow so that eventually they will become even more numerous than they were before the application of herbicides. To control these unwanted plants more and more chemicals have to be applied. Who gains by it? Only the chemical companies that manufacture herbicides.

Pesticides also affect insect pollinators that are responsible for the pollination of 80 percent of all plants. When we treat our fields with pesticides, most of these natural pollinators die in the process. And this not only reduces the yield of many agricultural crops but also jeopardizes the natural vegetation far away from the farm fields. To be more specific I shall cite one more example. As you know it is very hard to determine whether pesticides should be applied. Rodents have always been the main objects of extermination on farm fields. Polish zoologists have studied the life of field mice feeding on alfalfa. These mice destroy 23 to 24 percent of the alfalfa green mass. On the face of it the answer seems clear: destroy the mice so that alfalfa will grow undisturbed. Scientists, however, have noted two very particular aspects here. First, the plants that the mice nibble at sprout several shoots in the place of one shoot eaten. After that these shoots begin to bunch up and their growth process becomes more intense. Secondly, when they counted the amount of excrements that the mice introduce into the soil, they were surprised to see that these animals provide 78 percent of all necessary fertilizer. All this goes to show that it is necessary to maintain a limited mouse population in the field.

I have not yet spoken about the influence that pesticides have on man. What I have in mind is depression and irritability, disturbance of memory and abstract thinking, and so forth, as their side effects. Significantly, this is typical of organophosphates, one of the best developed modern pesticides. I would like to cite still another example so as to conclude our discussion about pesticides. Just a single contact a man has with certain pesticides, which causes no visible functional disturbance, brings about the disruption of the alpha rhythms of the brain, which lasts for about six months. We do not know yet what causes the disruption of the electrical activity of the brain as recorded in the encephalograms. One thing is clear: nothing good comes out of this one short contact.

Of course I could not touch upon all the problems of pesticides and take up only the most important of them. I would like to say in conclusion that traces of pesticides have been spotted in the organisms of ninety-six to ninety-nine human beings out of a hundred. It looks as if one-fifth of cancer incidence in people over forty-five years of age is linked directly with the presence of pesticides in their body. Very little is known yet about the harmful effect of pesticides, although our knowledge of them increases every year. It seems that society does not take a serious enough attitude to the utilization of these chemicals. Of all the pesticides being marketed in the United States only 38 percent have been checked for their carcinogenic effect, 40 percent for teratogenetic effect (causing monstrosity) and only 10 percent of the pesticides have been analyzed for their mutagenic effect (causing genetic changes). In the USSR, Britain, and other countries only about 10 percent of the permitted pesticides are open to detection in food, water, and in the natural environment in general. It looks as if the pesticides are the true Trojan horse of modern civilization.

RE You have given a shocking picture of the effect that pesticides have on all living things on Earth. Let us hope that it will be brought home to the broad masses as well. People must understand the tremendous destructive force inherent in all of what seem to be our insignificant actions, when these actions have a cumulative effect.

Of course something is being done to offset their side effects, but all that occurs sporadically. For example, the Swedish government has mandated the halving of the amount of insecticides applied in farming; this is a unique decision in world practice. The use of inhibitors in the fields also has been banned; most likely a ban will be put on the importation of crops produced by multinationals and requiring the application of pesticides. On the whole our ultimate goal should be banning the use of pesticides.

So far we have been talking mostly about the negligent treatment of soil. But we also manipulate the atmosphere. And this is no less serious a threat than despoliation of the fruit-bearing soil.

At the start of our meeting today we said that toxins are substances introduced in wrong places and at the wrong time. Toxins are also the product of wrong combinations. Strangely enough this applies to such a natural substance as ozone. The molecule of ozone consists of three atoms of oxygen. In its very small concentration ozone plays a tremendous role in the life of the Earth. Without the ozone filter in the stratosphere, there can be no higher organisms on our planet.

This is why we were greatly alarmed when we discovered that the ozone layer around the Earth was getting thinner. If the question at issue were some natural variations linked with the movement of air masses, the holes in the ozone layer would eventually be filled in. However, since the activity of man is so much a part of it, we are in for trouble. The opinion is gaining ground that the main culprits are chlorine and bromine discharged into outer space in the form of halogenic hydrocarbons, which we call freons. In the stratosphere freons act like some sort of predators that tear ozone molecules apart.

Many years ago the Committee on the Environment of the Royal Swedish Academy of Sciences suggested, with my participation, that the government ban the use of freons in aerosols. Each one of the aerosol sprays contains tiny doses of such freons, but taken together the amount of such freon becomes dangerous. Such a ban came into effect first in Sweden, with the United States and later some other countries following suit.

But what was the use of that? Scientists have discovered that there is a lot more freon in refrigerators, in foam rubber, in insulation materials, and so forth. The latest measurements taken from satellites have shown that the ozone layer is disintegrating much faster than it was originally believed, which is an ominous sign. The defects in the ozone layer today were originally caused by the freons that were released some thirty or even forty years ago. And if we continue to pump freons into the atmosphere, our children and grandchildren will reap the consequences.

What form will these consequences take? As far as I can understand, we have to draw our conclusions on more or less well-grounded assumptions. I believe everybody will agree that growing ultraviolet radiation from outer space will greatly increase the incidence of skin cancer. The Swedish scientist who was the first to raise the alarm over the freons in aerosol containers also warned that if we continued using them this way we would wear gloves and masks in the next century. Many people believe that intensive ultraviolet radiation will badly affect the genes, DNA. This radiation may also affect photosynthesis, with lasting effects on farm production. The climate, too, may change considerably.

A Y The Americans, who have a flair for counting, say that the incidence of skin cancer is already growing at the rate of 2 percent a year.

R E I have heard of that. Actually this is just one side of the problem, for clearly the insufficiency of ozone in the stratosphere is dangerous to life. However, its excess near the surface of the Earth is also harmful. Ozone, which is the product of solar radiation coming in contact with nitric oxides and hydrocarbons from car exhaust, may be instrumental in the destruction of trees in the forest.

The conclusion is that one should not manipulate natural substances in order either to reduce their amount to a minimum or to leave too much of them in the environment. More or less directed efforts are being made in the West to reduce the use of freon, but the resistance from the mighty commercial circles is still high. I do not think that this problem is any simpler in the Soviet Union. But you must know better.

A Y   This problem may even be more difficult in our country. When factories belch clouds of smoke and ashes that settle on our bodies and our clothes, they remind us that we should install filters. However, when we speak about long-term effects of our activities— something that neither a designer, nor a technologist, nor even a scientist can see, but which our children or grandchildren will come in contact with—the decision maker will find it extremely difficult to take prohibitive actions. In principle our centralized economy enables us, in our socialist society, to make any decision we find necessary. However, the insufficient ecologization of our thinking and a desire for quick returns make it difficult to take action that would serve long-term interests as well as short-term ones.

R E   Now a few words about another question concerning the atmosphere. What I have in mind is the growing accumulation of carbon dioxide in the air. Since this problem is extensively discussed in books and periodicals, it would be enough just to mention it while we are about it.

The climatologists of the East and West are of the opinion that any further concentration of carbon dioxide in the atmosphere may produce a hothouse effect that will radically change the Earth's climate in the next fifty or one hundred years. It is widely believed that in the middle of the next century the concentration of carbon dioxide in the northern hemisphere will double.

So far the belief has been that the climatic changes linked with the growing proportion of carbon dioxide in the atmosphere will continue to increase at a very low rate. Today there is a different view on the subject: at some moment that nobody can determine precisely the climate may change suddenly. There must be some sort of line of demarcation, but where and when it will pass, nobody knows for sure. But when we finally do find out, it will be much too late: there will be no way back for at least several generations. It may be many hundreds of years before the oceans absorb the excess of carbon dioxide.

We are playing a very dangerous game. The result may be sad.

A Y The problem of the so-called hothouse effect is possibly even more complicated than you have described. It has been established conclusively that over the past 100 years the annual rise of carbon dioxide in the atmosphere has been around 0.4 percent. Until recently everybody thought that this is the result of the burning of fossil fuel. However, the investigations carried out during the past decade have proved that even more carbon dioxide is discharged into the atmosphere by the decomposition of organic matter by microorganisms when the soil loses its forest cover. The once passive microorganisms become very active as the result not only of the felling of tropical trees but also the forests of the temperate zone. Unexpectedly, we began to notice a rise in the concentration not only of carbon dioxide but also the monoxides of nitrogen, methane, and ethane. Significantly, the concentration of carbon dioxide grows annually by 0.4 percent, as we said, whereas the annual concentration of methane and ethane is a whole 2 percent. It has lately been established that the rate of absorption of carbon dioxide by the ocean is much higher than previously thought. However, nobody has even suspected that so much methane is discharged into the atmosphere. Actually, to this day no one can understand where all this methane comes from. Some of the theories on this score are nothing short of fantasy. For example, it is presumed that intestinal microorganisms in termites are responsible for this. Termites are probably the only creatures capable of digesting cellulose because of the microorganisms living in their intestines. This process is attended by the discharge of methane. Is the high propagation of termites over the past years perhaps closely linked with the growing accumulation of methane in the atmosphere? This again points to our lack of knowledge. One thing is clear: we have caused a disruption in some natural process. What it is exactly we do not know, because we cannot reconstruct the chain of events to prove this.

R E But it is also believed that the proportion of methane in the atmosphere is going down because of the amelioration of swamps that give off considerable amounts of this important gas. However, it is clear that there are also other substances which, alongside carbon dioxide, stimulate the hothouse effect. Actually, carbon dioxide provides one of the most dismal illustrations of how we treat the Earth's resources.

For over one-and-a-half centuries we have been consuming prodigally the resources of coal and oil, which took millions of years to form out of the remnants of plants and animals. Carbon dioxide, which we have been discharging into the atmosphere over a comparatively short time from coal and oil deposits, is chiefly responsible for the hothouse effect that has frightened climatologists so much.

One Danish physicist has suggested this apt simile to put the problem in perspective. He said it is the same as collecting brushwood and twigs for a whole month and then burning them all up in a giant bonfire within four seconds. Momentary joy and sad consequences.

A Y   My famous countryman, professor Dmitri Mendeleev, who devised the periodic table of elements, said early in the twentieth century: "To use oil and coal for fuel is the same as to burn banknotes in an oven."

R E   I think we should touch upon still another form of "air attack," which over the past several years has taken precedence over all other environmental questions in both East and West.

What I have in mind is acid intoxication. While acid rains poured over lakes, rendering them lifeless, people felt rather indifferent about it. The water was getting more and more transparent, and death invisibly hovered over its glittering surface. When pine trees began to shed their needles, looking more and more like skeletons, we began to worry about intoxication that had set in imperceptibly long before we realized what was actually happening. After all, we think of trees as the symbols of life, and when they begin to wilt, this means that we are going to be affected, too.

We can speak about three aspects of acid intoxication. First for us, the dwellers of coniferous forests, acid intoxication shakes loose one of the principal foundations of our stable existence. Secondly, we may draw the conclusion that what is bad for foliage is most likely bad for the cells of the human organism. And, finally, the close proximity of our human species to nature has left somewhere inside us a nook of wilderness that we draw on for our spiritual health. When trees die, something in the "green zones" of our soul also begins to fade.

Since the acid rains have no political boundaries, the problem becomes truly international. It is not easy to come to terms with industrial enterprises. The enterprises in Country "A" say: we would be very happy to reduce the amounts of sulfur discharged, but we cannot do that because of competition with similar enterprises in Country "B." And you can hear the same being said in Country "B." Everything depends on the willingness and opportunities of governments to cooperate in this field.

In countries with a mixed economy, such as Sweden, we often have to fight against this irresponsible attitude of major enterprises to people and natural resources.

A Y Strangely enough we, in the Soviet Union, also come across such things. And we do that although we have no private enterprises.

R E The governments of countries with a mixed economy must set up some sort of protective net for people and their environment. A great deal may be created within a specific country, and indeed many things are being done there already. However, the dissemination of toxic substances across national boundaries and the stiff competition between countries call for international cooperation.

A Y It seems we have good results here. Suffice it to say that all European countries have signed a treaty on a 30 percent reduction in sulfur dioxide discharge into the atmosphere.

R E It is true. There is an international agreement on a reduction in 1993 of sulfur dioxide discharge by 30 percent below the level that existed in 1980. The so-called Club–30 has a membership of twenty countries, including Sweden and the Soviet Union.

A Y   If I am not mistaken, West Germany, which was not particularly enthusiastic about such agreements, took most stringent measures against sulfur dioxide discharge, especially after its own forests began to perish catastrophically. The plan in that country is to cut sulfur dioxide discharge by as high as 80 percent.

R E   This is very important. The southerly winds sweep the gaseous discharge from the continent toward Scandinavia. However, when the Norwegians and we Swedes first raised the question of acid intoxication of forests, the West Germans shrugged off our complaints as alarmist. The soils of West Germany are richer in lime, and this is why they acted initially as some sort of buffer zone. However, later this buffer zone lost much of its neutralizing effect. Intoxication of forests is a slow and almost imperceptible process up to a point. After that the process begins to develop more rapidly and now West Germany reacts to acid rains very painfully.

A Y   I have some absolutely astonishing figures. In 1907, 9,000 hectares of forest in West Germany, or one eight-hundredth part of its forestland, were affected by sulfur dioxide. By 1970 one-eightieth of its forests was contaminated. And in 1980 this figure stood at one-eighth. Today three-quarters of the forestland in the Federal Republic has been affected by acid rains.

R E   The West German government has formally admitted that the country has more than half of its forests affected in this way.
The figures may vary, which is not surprising. In the Alps, which have been particularly affected, 80 percent of the trees suffer from contamination, and in Schwarzwald three-quarters of the forestland are sick. At first only coniferous trees suffered, but now the contamination has spread to broadleaved forests as well. As a result, many areas in West Germany have become chemical deserts.
Actually, sulfur is not the only substance that causes acid intoxi-

cation. The nitrogen which is discharged in car exhausts is also very aggressive, and some researchers believe that at the end of this century it will cause even more harm than sulfur. The combined action of acid intoxication and carbon-dioxide intoxication is even stronger.

Most alarming is the growing acidity of the soil, a defect that will be very hard to correct if air pollution does not stop immediately. In Erzgebirge, which had beautiful forests until recently, the soil has become almost completely barren, with only some varieties of grass still growing. When the topsoil was removed in order to get down to the yet unharmed layer, scientists found that the intoxication had penetrated to a depth of half a meter. In my country, especially in areas closer to the "purveyors" of acid rains on the continent and in the British Isles, soil acidity has grown five to ten times over. The nutrient content has gone down over several decades by half. Many fields may soon be left without manganese and calcium (manganese molecules are called the "molecules of life" and they are essential for photosynthesis); the acid situation is also encroaching upon the groundwaters. What was previously considered impossible, due to soil resistivity, has become a reality.

It stands to reason that the denizens of the forest also suffer from acid rains. In Europe the most striking example is Czechoslovakia where brown coal is still used as fuel. The Czechs believe that acid intoxication has killed nine-tenths of the small animal population of their forests.

I would like to cite two more examples, one from a country in the West and the other from a country in the East, neither of them belonging to Club–30. In Western Europe the principal source of discharge of sulfur is Britain. In all the other countries of Western Europe sulfur discharge is on its way down while in Britain, by contrast, the amount of such discharge is growing. Scandinavia and the coastal countries of Europe are open to acid winds from the West. The governments of the northern countries have been strongly, albeit unsuccessfully, protesting against what we regard as "an affront to the windward countries." This cannot but afflict the natural environment, the people and the historical monuments in

Britain itself. Even in terms of the filthy lucre the country is a loser. The Scots, for example, see that their lakes are dying.

Poland to the east had tremendous problems connected with postwar reconstruction. This task was finally accomplished but now the Poles have to save the country again, this time because its industrial facilities discharge lots of sulfur dioxide, carbon dioxide, and nitric oxides. According to Polish scientists, the discharge of sulfur dioxide alone comes up to six million tons a year.

According to some more pessimistic forecasts, this figure will double by the year 2000. The four most contaminated areas have officially been declared zones of ecological disaster. One such zone is Kraków, known as one of the ancient cultural centers of Europe. Warsaw was destroyed by the war, but Kraków was spared this fate. But today it is open to air attacks from its own factories, and the acrid gases are eating into its sculptures one millimeter after another. I have seen some figures provided by Poland itself, if I remember correctly. These figures say that three-quarters of Poland's land area has been contaminated in one way or another. This also affects both vegetation and people: infant mortality is growing, life expectancy is going down, the incidence of cancer, blood disease, respiratory disorders, and so forth, is growing too.

I have chosen these examples to show the seriousness of the situation. In one way or another this applies to all countries. Western Europe can feel it very keenly. The ecological tragedy for the Poles is also a disaster for their neighbors. Our housekeeping is still far from perfect. However, I think that the countries of the West, except Britain, are behind Eastern Europe for the amount of atmospheric and soil pollution. The Swedish minister for environmental protection has called upon such countries as Poland, the German Democratic Republic, and the Soviet Union to change their ecological thinking in order to reduce the harm inflicted upon the environment in Europe. I can imagine what a huge problem it is for your country.

AY This surely is a very important problem. But I want to add in this connection that the Poles themselves are very much concerned by what is happening. I have been to Poland, including Kraków, several times and know how worried the Poles are about the state of their environment.

We, here in our country, are taking strong measures to reduce the sulfur discharge into the atmosphere. I think that about 40 percent of the funds allocated in the USSR for environmental purposes go for the development and installation of air filters. Our specialists say (and this has been made public in the Soviet press) that, despite industrial progress, we have succeeded in halting the spread of atmospheric pollution. However, the level at which this has been achieved exceeds the permissible level in the industrially advanced regions of the world. Incidentally, I must add here that much of the atmospheric pollution comes to my country with the westerly winds blowing from Czechoslovakia, Poland, and West Germany. Among the Soviet republics that suffer from such acid-laden winds is Byelorussia, which does not have an extensive industry of its own. The prevailing easterly winds carry off most of the pollutants from the central regions to the regions with a relatively sparse population. This relieves the situation somewhat. We disperse locally generated pollutants over a vast territory, and nature somehow manages to cope with it.

R E And what about the taiga?

A Y In some areas, especially around major industrial centers of Siberia, the taiga is in a very poor state of preservation. This can well be seen from outer space. The very fact that my country has joined Club–30 shows that our statesmen have begun to treat this problem seriously.

However, as a biologist, I think that the approach to this problem is again not sufficiently ecological. We are trying to neutralize the discharge by setting up filters. This, of course, is a half measure. Actually, the radical solution here would be the creation of waste-free production. I am no specialist in this field, but I have heard that France has set a good example by stopping any further importation of sulfur because it obtains all the sulfur it needs from her smoke-stacks, so to speak. The ecologically sound approach is not to purify the air, but not to pollute it.

RE According to experts, the sulfur dioxide discharge should be reduced by 30 percent. I think this figure was named because the rate of reduction was dictated by people who are clearly very slow on the uptake. But actually it would be possible to reduce the waste discharge by 80 percent.

To my mind, when the question at issue is the environment, people too readily agree to make compromises. This may serve the goals of practical policy, but a person who is really concerned about the situation may see through it a rejection of what is truly valuable.

It is not sufficient to make some isolated adjustments. To save our part of the world, its forests, land, waters, and people, it is necessary to take more resolute measures than those implemented so far.

AY Are you talking about Europe?

RE Precisely. We have technical facilities and more are in the pipeline. So there is no hitch there. The main problem is that we do not go beyond counting the rubles, kronor, marks, or pounds sterling required for their utilization. The narrowness of this approach is evident because even a rough assessment of the environment shows that the destruction of the environment is much more costly than the building of the most sophisticated and expensive purification facilities. This means that a healthy ecology is a healthy economy even if reckoned in purely monetary terms.

AY This example shows that ecology is closely associated not only with the economy but also with politics. None of the countries can on their own solve this problem: all of us are linked together. You singled out Britain and Poland as countries that do not belong to Club–30. There are, of course, political and economic reasons for it. I am convinced that the domestic difficulties in Poland of the past several years have greatly impeded the solution of the problem of nature protection and have prevented Poland's entry into Club–30. All of its economy was rocked by internal problems. Britain, as you know, has a higher level of unemployment and its economy is more strained than in some other countries of Western Europe, notably Sweden and West Germany. The purely psychological aspect of this problem is also important: their forests have been damaged to a much lesser extent because only an infinitesimal part of sulfur from North America reaches these countries. All problems are interlinked: economic, ecological, political, and psychological.

RE Speaking of the economy you mean its financial aspect. Actually, the true capital of any country is its natural resources. With some areas of Poland being so badly polluted that its population should in all justice be evacuated, how could all this be compared with the zlotys that go into the building of purification facilities?

AY But Poland does not have these zlotys.

RE This is why I want to go back to what I mentioned in a different connection. Why not set up an international foundation that would allocate funds for zones of ecological disaster in countries whose governments cannot cope with the problem? Such assistance to one region may also benefit others.

I think it's necessary to radically change the thinking of both individuals and governments with regard to these problems. The question is not about how many zlotys, rubles, or kronor a certain ecological operation may cost, but how many zlotys, rubles, or kronor we would have to pay for our inaction.

AY You are quite right. It is thinking ecologically, and not the zlotys or kronor, that can save the situation. Some time ago I read an interesting news item: a local council in the western Urals banned utilization of defoliants in the forests of its territory, because the

gain the forest rangers derived from stimulating the growth of coniferous trees was far below the cost of the damage thus inflicted
upon the natural environment. Although the forest rangers expected to reap high profits in a few years, and the damage they
would cause the environment would make itself felt for many years,
the local population opted for the environment. This is a good example of ecological thinking. It is a pity, though, that examples
such as this one are still few and far between, and that it was ad-
dressed at the level of a local administrative council alone.

R E We have already spoken about how nitric fertilizers can kill a lake
and how acid rains kill life at its very source.

However, contamination of water is not limited to the nitric discharge and acid rains. For us, Homo technicus, water has become a
place for the dumping and transportation of waste material of an
industrial society. There is no such reservoir, even the ocean, that is
large enough to cope with pollutants. In many places the growing
mountains of waste and refuse poison groundwaters.

In some places initial purification operations are carried out to
keep down water pollution. But even well-purified water often contains many stable chemical compounds mainly of industrial origin.
I am convinced that this problem can be solved by, for example,
introducing closed cycles.

It is very sad to see large industrial enterprises still dumping
poisonous waste into rivers and seas. Some do not stop at shipping
such wastes out to the North Sea and burning them up.

A Y But how do they do that? Right out at sea?

R E Yes, in vessels specially equipped for this purpose. One West German vessel flying a Belgian flag of convenience and two U.S. ships
under a Liberian flag make shuttle trips, carrying toxic wastes that
nobody wants to dispose of on land.

A Y Do they burn them up right on board?

RE   Precisely. They burn up the toxic wastes in special incinerators installed on board. The smoke containing dioxides and other toxic
substances stretches out over the sea, while the poisonous ashes are
dumped right into the water. Oceanologists carry on scientific studies in the North Sea, and many maritime nations have signed a
convention [Baltic Sea Marine Mammal Convention] for its protection. Yet, as far as I know, this is the only sea in the world where
the burning of industrial and other wastes is allowed. Green Peace
is out to put an end to this absurd practice. At least it has succeeded
in calling public attention to it. Meanwhile, one preposterous action follows another that makes you wonder what this world of ours
is coming to. I have read, for instance, that the British are planning to sink their obsolete atomic submarines in the depths of the
North Sea.

AY   We have already touched upon the problem of water, including surface water. To the ecological troubles you have mentioned I shall
add one that we spoke about earlier on. What I have in mind is the
pollution of water reservoirs with agricultural effluence. We are not
without sin here either, and many of our rivers are very badly polluted. Every year toxic substances are accidentally dumped into rivers. These emissions may not be as massive as the one on the Rhine
in 1987. Nevertheless, they arouse the growing concern of the population of the whole region.

In this troubled situation we somehow always seek some sort of
bright moment. Any river starts out with a spring, a tiny source of
water. So, over the past five years a new movement in defense
of small rivers was initiated and is gaining momentum in the European part of the Soviet Union. This movement is not always successful; nevertheless it has some achievements to its credit. The participants in the movement have restored some wellsprings and have
planted trees around small rivers. As a result, fish are coming back
to the rivers, and the surrounding wilderness attracts more and
more animals and birds that have long since vanished in these parts.

And now I would like to mention other dangers lurking not only in rivers, but also in the air, dangers that for some reason we do not give much thought to.

RE I want to add just a few more words about water, that wonderful liquid which we think is so plentiful when we sail across the ocean, but which would amount to a mere few drops if our planet were the size of an apple.

There are good examples of successful purification of polluted rivers and lakes. Water, especially running water, has a marvelous capacity for self-cure if it is not under too much anthropogenic pressure. The industrial countries would make an unforgivable mistake if they did not use the existing purification technology.

But we are also responsible for the Third World where mostly only one person out of five in rural areas can use good drinking water. The very thought of many rivers teeming with bacteria and other harmful things that cause intestinal troubles is horrifying. Significantly, bacterial contamination is spreading to groundwater, too. According to international statistics, in many places of our planet 80 percent of diseases are caused by contaminated water and poor sanitary conditions. Every year millions of children die of dysentery, typhoid fever, diarrhea, helminthiasis carried by the same water that must be the vehicle of life, not death.

To solve this problem is the task of the world community, especially the rich countries. Actually it is quite possible that every family in the Third World will have drinking water either from a house tap or from a hydrant.

At the start of our dialogue we spoke about victims of war. However, from the point of view of morals, there is no difference between people killed by weapons or those killed by famine and water pollution, and that solely because society spends money on weapons, and not on humanitarian aid.

AY As a biologist I would like to say here that the principal role in self-purification of water is played by various living organisms in it: microorganisms, mollusks, mosquito larvae, and so forth. The famous cleanliness of Baikal water is largely the result of the fact that its entire mass goes through billions of tiny crayfish, called epishurs, three times a year. Every such crayfish is, at best, a mere millimeter long. So when we speak about the troubles that come from agricultural mismanagement, from soil pollution, we immediately associate them with the state of the living organisms in the soil that make water clean.

You, Rolf, are quite right that we are well equipped to purify water. Water is a renewable resource and we must provide all people on Earth with fresh water.

RE Regrettably, these problems also concern many families in the industrial countries. In some areas of West Germany the authorities warn the parents of newly born babies against using water from the tap because it contains nitric compounds to which infants are particularly sensitive. At the Hygiene Institute in Leipzig mothers are advised to cook baby food using mineral water. Just a reminder that the vast water problem in the Third World also exists in the developed world although on a smaller scale.

AY And yet it is serious all right.

RE It is immeasurably more serious in the Third World, because the problem affects millions of children and adults there.

AY I think we should now talk about things we have not discussed yet, but which I think would be wrong to ignore altogether in the context of our general analysis of the natural environment.

One such problem is the massive presence of electromagnetic fields in the atmosphere. Our knowledge of them is inadequate and we have rather scant information about the effect that radio waves have on the living world and on man in particular. What we do know, however, is very worrisome. If we irradiate rats with microwaves of the same intensity as exists around big radio stations, they will soon develop embryonic deviations leading to smaller litters and weaker progeny. The same effect on monkeys shows that a similar level of microwave irradiation modifies their behavior, making them irritable. There are also many psychic aberrations. The effect of electromagnetic fields on rats and rabbits weakens their immunity and they become susceptible to most common diseases. This is possibly why the residents of cities and industrial centers suddenly feel worse, and their mood changes, too.

About one percent of the population of the United States lives in areas with a dangerous level of electromagnetic radiation. And about 20 percent of the entire population of the developed countries—in both East and West—live in areas where electromagnetic radiation makes itself felt though it is below danger level.

Of course, there are still many things we do not know about. However, we do know that electromagnetic modes induced by the movement of a trolley bus or a tram can be recorded by instruments over a distance of several kilometers. We also know that these waves are very similar to those of the electromagnetic activity of the brain. And we know that living organisms are by far more sensitive than our as yet imperfect recording instruments. There are some well-established facts about the effect of electromagnetic waves on living organisms. For example, on their way upstream in the Volga the spawning sturgeons stop as if before an invisible barrier at a point where high voltage power lines are stretched over the river. It is well known that under high-voltage power lines the animal population is different than in surrounding areas. The flowers growing here may include more deviant specimens. There are unconfirmed reports that the effects of this electromagnetic radiation, like the effects of nuclear radiation and the action of pesticides, may be cumulative.

I shall illustrate some more dangerous effects on nature that have so far gone almost unnoticed. First about so-called light pollution. Those who flew in an airplane over populated centers at night may have seen a tremendous stream of light coming from big cities. When in summer I am not away on an expedition, I often live in my country home about seventy kilometers from Moscow. After dark I notice a glow of light in the direction of Moscow. Experiments with birds and other animals have shown that the disruption of the light regime may also disrupt the rhythm of propagation and other physiological processes. It is not yet clear how specifically this affects the human being, but affect us it does.

Next comes noise pollution. An experimental group of rats was exposed to the noise of the New York subway for two hours a day over a period of a month. After that the males could not fertilize the females and many females became either barren or produced smaller litters of rats. The greatest manmade noise comes from the U.S. space shuttles. When a shuttle takes off from the California shore, the noise of its engines causes spontaneous births in the seals living on neighboring islands. At the request of American biologists the shuttle program was later modified in order to preserve the seal population. Needless to say that noise also affects man. Very possibly loud noise is not currently as dangerous as pesticides or other chemical agents, but nevertheless it brings about serious disruptions in our environment, causing additional stresses and strains.

Another unpleasant phenomenon is dust pollution. The residents of big cities have forever to grapple with dust accumulations in their apartments. In Sweden, for example, 500 kilograms of dust settle down on one hectare of territory, and in Belgium 6,000 kilograms. This dust contains many harmful substances and microorganisms. Scientists have made no serious practical study of it yet. Dust is a major problem. And although it is not as bad as chemical pollution, dust makes our life less comfortable.

There are so many different factors in the world that have a bad effect on the human being that I really cannot enumerate them all. One of the products of technical progress is plastics that require the use of large amounts of polycholorinated biphenyls (PCB). It is now known that PCB may cause the death of newborn babies. For macaque monkeys 2.5 milligrams of PCB per kilogram of body weight has a marked effect on their propagation. One kilogram of the milk of nursing mothers in the United States sometimes contains up to 10 milligrams of PCB. Swedish researchers have shown that seals in the Baltic have stopped propagating mainly because their organisms have accumulated too much PCB. Usually, 90 percent of seal females get pregnant, but in the Gulf of Bothnia this figure has been reduced to a mere 25 percent.

RE One of the reasons for this is the fact that heavily contaminated water causes adhesion of the walls of their uteri, thus preventing the seals from bringing forth their progeny.

AY This is exactly what I wanted to say just now: out of ten pregnant females only one can give birth normally. Danger lurks everywhere, in the most unexpected places. Disinfectant soap containing hexachlorophene was once very popular in Sweden and other countries. This is a very effective disinfectant. But later it turned out that the medical nurses who washed their hands more than ten times a day, gave birth to children who in 16 percent of the cases had genetic deviations. We are not yet familiar with many existing chains of interaction. However, we know that over the past fifteen years the number of children with psychic and physical defects has grown several times over. In our country alone people living in houses built near motorways have a statistically higher cancer incidence than those living in houses more than 50 meters away from these roads. The statistics on West Germany, Britain, and the United States show that the growing amounts of lead in blood results in mental retardation. It has been proven that our contemporaries have from 100 to 1,000 times as much lead as the mummified bodies of people who lived in the remote past.

It is very hard to predict how this or that new pollutant will affect different animals and plants. Some plants, for example, are twenty-five to thirty times as sensitive to benzol as man. Fish have proved to be more vulnerable to many pesticides than mammals. Chickens are more sensitive to some pesticides than rats.

Nobody can analyze ahead of time the innumerable combinations of substances we introduce into the biosphere. This is why we cannot predict what reaction this or that substance will have. The problem is all the more complicated since about a thousand new chemicals are dumped onto the world market. There are new factors, too, such as the laser beam that did not exist in the past. Our environment is in a very unstable condition and we do not know what is in store for it over the long-term.

RE You say that there is a thousand times more lead in the blood of the modern man than there was in ancient mummies. Recent analyses of the ice in Greenland showed that a ton of fresh ice and snow contains ten times as much lead as a ton of ice two hundred years old. The blood of a Swede, and I think that the same can be said about a Russian, contains ten times as much lead as a resident of a nonindustrialized country. The intestinal tract of a child absorbs ten times as much lead as that of an adult. According to the doctors, lead prevents normal formation of hemoglobin and retards mental development.

One of the sources of lead is exhaust fumes. Small children are particularly susceptible because their respiratory organs are at the level of exhaust pipes.

On the whole children get the worst of pollution simply because they are more vulnerable to it than adults. The liver of a baby, for example, cannot cope with nitric compounds as does the liver of a grown-up person. Cases are known of a baby dying suddenly without any distinctive symptoms of a disease. They just stop breathing, the only possible cause being air pollution.

The children and adolescents living today are the first generation growing in an environment filled with chemicals. They have come up against an absolutely new problem in the history of human society. According to physicians (I am referring to them again for better authority), somewhere between 10 and 30 percent of children in the industrial countries are affected by environmental pollution.

But about the most dismal aspect of environmental destruction is the sins of parents against their children. As we said earlier, children are in danger already at the very moment of conception, and even before conception. According to a Norwegian researcher, the proportion of productive spermatozoids in Scandinavian men dropped from 70-odd percent in 1966 to 30-odd percent in 1986. If this is true, the question at issue is not merely a phenomenon that concerns Scandinavia alone. Some researchers are of the opinion that by the end of this century the number of infertile men will have grown considerably, should this tendency persist in the future. Could it be that nature has rebelled against a species that is so recklessly destroying the very foundations of life on Earth?

A Y Similar studies have been carried out in the United States. Their results are largely the same, although figures somewhat differ.

Here we spoke a great deal about terrible, dangerous, or simply unpleasant environmental effects on man, on living nature. It looks like the man who lived early in this century did not have nearly as many unpleasant things to deal with as those we have today. The environment is changing quickly in directions that are very dangerous for all of us. Nevertheless we, people who are routinely exposed to these environmental changes, do not see them as they come. A good example of that is the following experiment. A frog was placed in a saucepan filled with water that was then put over a flame. The frog died in the hot water without so much as trying to jump out. But if you heat the water without the frog and put it into the hot water, it will be mustering all its strength to jump out. Humankind must do its utmost not to find itself in a situation similar to that of the first frog.

R E I fully share your fears, Alexei. But we must note that more and more people are getting increasingly concerned with environmental problems. In most countries of Western Europe the movement for environmental protection is gaining momentum, and although it is not yet strong enough, political leaders have to reckon with it.

As far as I understand, a similar movement is gaining ground in the Soviet Union. The outstanding writer Valentin Rasputin, scientists such as you, Alexei, and many of your colleagues, are pooling their efforts to consolidate ecological thinking at all levels. In some cases you have succeeded in changing the course of events.

A movement which is not constrained by national boundaries is on the rise, a movement that will hopefully grow stronger.

I shall cite still another example of environmental toxic pollution. Most of us very possibly do not even think about much of our cultural heritage falling apart. The toxic fumes carried by streams of air erode the outstanding works of art of ancient Greece and Rome, mutilate architectural monuments. I have already mentioned Kraków and its ecological troubles. Everywhere environmental pollution erodes unique architectural structures, memorials, and statuary at frightening speed. Many of these works of culture are changing beyond recognition.

Water can be purified sufficiently well if we decide to apply the technology we have at our disposal, and if we direct our intellect and energy toward developing new methods. It is also possible that future generations will enjoy the forests that have vanished from large parts of our territory, if we remove the source of evil instead of taking half-way measures.

But the eroded ancient marble goddesses, emperors, and apostles will never regain their pristine beauty. Works of art are perishing. Part of our common European heritage is going to waste, and the future generations will lose some of their history. This is also an important element of the wider problem of environmental pollution.

A Y You are quite right saying that over the past several years public opinion has been growing in favor of environmental protection. I have in hand the results of a public opinion poll carried out in many European countries between 1979 and 1986. In most of them environmental protection rated among the two or three top-priority issues. In all countries (except Ireland) the better part of the population thinks that environmental protection must be put before the problem of economic growth. In most countries 59 or 60 percent of the population was overwhelmingly worried by the prodigal waste of global resources. I think we shall accomplish our task if this percentage grows somewhat after the publication of our discussion.

R E And this means that we must in the final analysis find a way to curb those who poison everything around, those who defy public opinion and national frontiers.

Over the past several years the United States and the European countries have been gradually stiffening the rules for handling toxins. As a result they have banned the use of certain chemicals. However, many big chemical enterprises that show absolutely no compunction when it comes to profit making have turned the Third World into a profitable market for toxins banned in their home countries.

The British journal, the *Ecologist*, which has done a lot to expose this sort of activity, gives the names of a large number of enterprises that have found a way to circumvent the stringent rules at home by exporting chemical components that are then put together in the countries of the Third World where workers receive very low wages and where safety and sanitary control is practically nonexistent. The highly toxic preparations are then put on sale under a new label, in spite of the fact that some of them induce cancer or infertility.

Some toxins that are banned in the United States are used for spraying banana and citrus plantations in Central America. In some "banana republics" the fruits are thus treated three times: workers spray each separate plant; after that airplanes spray them with toxic chemicals, some of which get into adjacent reservoirs; and finally packaging women workers apply more chemicals with their bare hands. According to the *Ecologist*, every minute someone in the Third World gets poisoned by these chemicals, and every hundred minutes one person dies of contamination.

To stop the ecogangsters is a global problem.

A Y As a westerner you understand this situation better than I. As is known, 95 percent of trade in raw materials with the developing countries is in the hands of multinational corporations. Of course, these corporations have a stake in cutting down the price of raw materials and, conversely, in raising the price of their own products as much as possible. Thus the raw materials come to the multinationals cheaply. No wonder that this leads to impoverishment of the Third World countries.

And there is another aspect of the activities of the multinational corporations. They sell high-grade grain on condition that the buyers will treat this grain with pesticides bought from the same corporations. I know for a fact that the agents that promote the sale of pesticides from these multinational corporations are sometimes paid twice as much money as the scientists who develop pesticide-free farming methods. These rich corporations often spend big money in a way that can hardly be called honest.

I have read articles in the American press about the analysis of the activity of a major private pesticides testing laboratory (Industrial Biotest Laboratory). The question of whether it is possible to apply the pesticides is decided on the basis of its reports. This laboratory has submitted to the government 22,000 reports confirming the safety of the pesticides in question. However, most of these reports (80 percent) have been falsified. Based on these fraudulent reports, 25 percent of the pesticides are sold to Canada and Malaysia. It is clear that someone must have done it on purpose.

RE What you are saying about falsified data is something I never heard about. But when you tell me about a situation that cries out to heaven, something I can actually see with my own eyes, I ask myself: maybe we should have pulled the cord of the emergency brake some twenty years ago. After all, the ecological conditions in the industrial countries were quite decent in those days. We could have put greater emphasis on quality rather than on quantity. One concerned Swedish ecologist, Professor Torset Hägerstrand, had this to say about the situation in the world: "It looks as if we were whirling around in the merry-go-round of technical progress with no control over its consequences."

With every passing decade we find it increasingly difficult to exercise control over these consequences. But this is exactly what we should achieve. We must learn how to say "no" to technologies baneful for the environment and for human beings. We must develop favorable alternatives to the existing technologies. We must visualize the make-up of a society that we want to leave to our children. We must be ready to pay money and give up what is wasteful and unimportant in order to achieve a cleaner environment. The fundamental decision that we will yet have to make can be summed up in these words: "no production should harm nature!"

A Y How illusory is material well-being if it is to be achieved in developed countries such as West Germany at the cost of the loss of three-quarters of its forestland, by risking the health of our children drinking water from the tap. This, I think, is the right time to put on the brakes and revise all of our present priorities.

R E I feel I have gained a lot from our exchange of views here in Moscow. Now I am looking forward to meeting you in Stockholm where we shall continue our dialog.

DAY 5

MAN IS PART OF NATURE, WHICH I'D LIKE TO
TALK ABOUT MORE AT LENGTH. BUT MAN IS
BOTH A REMARKABLE AND EVIL PART OF NATURE.

—ALEXEI YABLOKOV

ONCE MAN CAME TO REALIZE THE POSSIBILITIES
OF HIS BRAIN HE BECAME CONFIDENT OF
HIMSELF, INDEED TOO MUCH SO. ENCHANTED
BY THE NEW POSSIBILITIES NOW OPEN TO HIM,
HE FAILED TO SEE THE DELUSIONS
OF HIS OWN MIND.

—ROLF EDBERG

■

R E Welcome to Sweden, Alexei. Welcome to Stockholm and our Academy of Sciences!

Since we met in Moscow the trees have shed their leaves and their branches look like roots on the grounds around the beautiful building of the Academy.

In the course of our dialogue in Moscow we discussed the "botany of the modern world," as it were, and all those many things that threaten life on Earth and that are moving toward their critical threshold so well synchronized it's terrifying. I wonder what forces are at work within our own species that have brought us to this situation? Maybe we should give more thought to these questions so we can better understand the problems of our day and take a look at the future.

But before we turn to this theme I would like to hear more about your latest trip to the United States. As far as I understand, you took a keen interest in some desert island in the Pacific, "desert" in the sense that it has no people living there. What caused you to set out to the other end of the world to visit an insular rock somewhere far away in the West? Was it just an attempt to take refuge from our noisy, suffocating industrial society, or was it something that has a bearing on the subject at hand?

A Y After we parted in Moscow I spent a month in the United States in order to study the boundaries and structures of marine mammal populations that have been placed under special protection. I was busy developing new and more humane methods of studying seals and dolphins and had an opportunity to live on a desert island off

Los Angeles. It was really amazing and somehow illogical: a deserted island, seals, and the ocean on the one side, and the teeming human anthill of a giant city on the other. You may have heard about some incredible things happening in California: motorists shooting at one another on interstates. I did not believe it at first. But when I had spent three hours in a car, and saw all around me nothing but cars—six rows of them on my one side and four rows on the other, crawling at the speed of fifty meters a minute, I asked my American friend: "Do you have a pistol in the car?" The world is becoming more and more inhuman, misanthropic.

R E   I think we should have a separate discussion about humanism and morals. And what impression do you have of modern America?

A Y   I met there many people who, just like you and me, think about the future of man and nature. And all such meetings confirmed in me the conviction that the role of all concerned and thinking people, and not only scientists, is growing. It would be impermissible to allow only professional politicians to think about the fate of our world. The time has come when all people who are concerned about the future of their children and grandchildren should have a say in the matter and make themselves heard.

R E   Last year I visited Los Angeles and Tokyo. I must say that I also felt uneasy when I found myself caught up in the dizzying traffic. It is true, though, that I heard pistol shots only in the Hollywood film studios. But there was another thing I noticed. In both these huge cities the air is now much less polluted than it used to be. Los Angeles is now clear of yellow smog and the Tokyo policemen have an easier time of it. Both the Americans and Japanese, ten years before the Europeans, who are slow-starters, installed catalytic converters for car exhaust. This took almost immediate effect.

A prominent part in decision making of this sort is played by the public. Rachel Carson was the first. She was followed by Lester Brown, Barry Commoner, Ralph Nader, René DuBois, and Norman Mailer. Their statements aroused public sentiment and eventually led to measures to prevent the situation from becoming completely unbearable.

A Y It is true that the air in Los Angeles has become better. The change is dramatic if you compare the air in Los Angeles today with what it was like ten years ago. But there is another worrisome point. The natural environment over the better part of the highway from San Diego to Los Angeles was largely intact whereas now the area is cluttered with houses. And somewhere between the two cities I saw a giant, odd-shaped, arching structure, about 100 meters tall: a new atomic power station. It put me in mind of Chernobyl and of the incalculable damage that just one accident at such a station can bring. And along the beautiful Californian coast, with its surviving whales, dolphins, seals, and sea otters, I saw oil derricks that had not been there before. They stand both near the coast and far out on the horizon. Nature is rapidly retreating under our pressure. I am convinced that this retreat could bring most unpleasant things to humankind.

R E Nature suffers everywhere, though to a different extent. Sweden's second largest city, Göteborg, is not Los Angeles by far. And our shores in Skagerrak strait are not the Californian coast. Nevertheless our minister for the environment who recently visited Göteborg considered it necessary to set up a commission under the chairmanship of one of the leaders of the Green Peace movement with the idea of drawing up an emergency program for saving the natural environment in this part of Sweden, which she proclaimed a zone of intensive protection.

Sure, there is not one single country in the world that is free from ecological problems.

A Y As for me, I feel elated every time I go to Sweden whose environmental conditions may well be envied by any European nation. Of course, I know of the acid rains and of the dead forests and lakes. We have already talked about that. And yet ecologically Sweden seems to be a lot better off than, for example, many regions of the

European part of my own country. Stockholm, although it is a large modern city, retains many wooded areas, green lawns and fields, and clean water reservoirs. And even the Academy building where we are now stands in what looks like a small park.

RE It is true that by tradition our Academy devotes a great deal of attention to environmental protection. It even has a committee that is very active in this respect. Significantly, the Academy has instituted a prestigious international prize: "Pro mundi habitabili" (for a habitable world).

One of the founders of the Academy 250 years ago, and its first president, was Carl von Linné [better known as Linnaeus]. The first internationalist in this country, which in those days was in the backyard of civilized Europe, he corresponded with some seventy naturalists in other countries, exchanged seeds and plants with them and dispatched his pupils to all parts of the world so they could describe and take home plant species from other lands for his future study of plant life of the world. Incidentally, the Russian Empress Catherine sent him seeds for the part of Linné's botanical gardens that he called "Siberia."

Being a great lover of nature, Linné largely anticipated the judgments and conclusions made by the ecologists of our day about the need to protect nature and conserve its environment. He had a deeper insight into the integrated character of nature as a whole.

Linné regarded nature not only as a scene of merciless struggle for existence, but also as a model of interaction. In it every species existed not only for itself, but also for other species. It either is eaten by other living creatures or keeps them under control. In one of his most remarkable works he describes all living things as endowed with the function of "the policeman of nature." Every creature is under the supervision of some other creature and each plant or animal species has its own supervisor that keeps an eye on it so that it does not expand too much and crowd out the others. And this means that if even one such supervisor drops out, the balance is upset, which is fraught with disaster. But to serve one species in this way is to serve all. That, in Linné's view, is the overriding principle of nature, which was formulated long before the concept of "ecology" came into existence. Very possibly, the ideas that Linné formulated 250 years ago could serve as a good starting point for some considerations relevant to our times about the role and possibilities of man in this world.

As an ecologist you must have made a thorough study of the place that man as an organism holds among countless other organisms.

AY I am very pleased that we can continue our dialogue in Sweden, Linné's home country. Linné, of whom you speak with so much enthusiasm, is one of the greatest naturalists of all times.

Several years ago I was in Uppsala and then I wandered around the house where Linné had once lived. I tried to understand the sources of that man's genius who had shouldered the burden of the task that before him only very few people, starting with Aristotle, sought to resolve: to take all living things down to a system, to understand and encompass all living nature, to comprehend nature and the place that man holds in it. Linné performed a feat of heroism in science. Two hundred and fifty years ago, when everybody thought that man was the creation of God, Linné showed unequivocally the place of man in the system of nature and, consequently, the links between man and nature.

Since the issue of Linné's book, *The Systems of Nature*, man has acquired a formal status, "the rights of citizenship" within our system of knowledge. This great service that Swedish science has rendered to the world in the person of the great naturalist Carl Linné will never be forgotten. And now I shall attempt to formulate our modern scientific attitude to the question: what is man's place in the system of nature today?

This is no easy question. Sometimes I think it's easier to tell about those dangers that modern civilization has brought upon man and nature than to understand how all this has happened. All those numerous misfortunes that have come down upon modern civilization and those global problems we are beset with on all sides are undoubtedly associated with the origin of man. Man is part of nature, which I would like to talk about more at length. But man is both a remarkable and evil part of nature. Man's ability to work and to create something new has led to the unprecedented progress and development of human society. This is one side of the coin. But on the other, this ability has created all our modern problems.

Man's brain and man's hands are the products of biological evolution, evolution of living nature. At every stage of this evolution, at every moment of the four to five million years of the human race's formation, man's features and physical characteristics have been developing by natural selection, each one of them serving a purpose the way it does. For instance, the narrow eyes of the nomads of the desert are fashioned in a way that protects them from sand and dust, from wind and bright sun; the black skin serves to offset the dangerous ultraviolet solar radiation in the tropics; the long nose of some people and the short nose of others, large ears, long or short fingers—all that has emerged in the course of natural evolution, and has taken shape by selection.

But when it comes to the human brain we find ourselves somewhat puzzled. All we know about it suggests that the brain is a remarkable and extraordinary organ. There are many things about the brain that we still don't know, and its potential is not clear. It goes without saying that the human brain, too, has been created in the process of natural selection. But what forces have brought to life this organ with its largely unrealized potential, an organ which has no parallel in the entire animal world (possibly with the exception of some cetaceans)? What was the direction of natural selection that has led to the creation of this superpowerful instrument for the cognition of matter?

RE Following up this idea I would like to discuss why it happens that the human brain—this extraordinary instrument, as you say—fits so well the role that man has assumed in this world.

But before I go on I would like to dwell on what links us with all the other organisms which, just like us, depend for their existence on our planet, our home in the universe.

Strangely enough we came to understand our biological origin only in the middle of the last century. As is known, this happened when Charles Darwin continued Linné's work to determine man's biological status in nature and when he showed that our evolution is part of the evolution of all living things on Earth. We saw how in the never-ending process of creation, new species have emerged and old species have modified and adjusted to the ever changing conditions. We found a material for a new picture of the world, the material that has replaced the old myths about our origin.

One of the most remarkable results of this research is the fact that, by following in the footsteps of Linné and Darwin, the scientists of our time are pushing farther and farther back the threshold of time when life first emerged on our planet. Recently, scientists discovered inside the rock material of the African continent, which is some 3.4 billion years old, petrified microorganisms that contained, by all indications, the same complex chemical compounds that we see in the cells of the human body. This reminded us that all living organisms are built of similar elements, and that it took gigantic periods of time for evolution to take its course and create the forms of life that exist on Earth today.

A Y Modern science affirms that man originated as the result of the evolution of living nature. And the more profound our understanding of man, the more similarity we see between him and the rest of living things. In the structure of his molecules, in physiological and chemical reactions taking place in his organs and cells, man does not differ from other living creatures. Many celebrated scientists believe that life may not have originated on Earth but could be brought here from elsewhere in the universe. That might be so. But as for man, he emerged on Earth, and there is no doubt about it! He emerged from those primeval conditions that took shape on Earth in one way or another.

R E Hypotheses that life might have come to Earth from outside are sometimes advanced not only by the authors of science-fiction novels but also by quite serious scientists. At the turn of our century the Swedish astronomer Gustaf Arrhenius came up with a hypothe-

sis that life began as microspores that had come to Earth from outer
space in a stream of meteoric dust. Several years ago two other as-
tronomers postulated that living cells or fragments of living cells
could be found in the nuclei of comets. However, we are quite satisfied to know that man, just like any other organism, consists of
the chemical elements found on Earth.

And these are the elements that continue their wanderings
through our organism. The ancient myths and philosophical concepts brought forth the idea of universal circulation of matter. Modern science (and you are a representative of it) has given a new di-
mension to these mythical concepts and done it in a way that is
fascinating to the nonspecialist. Today we can see such rotation at
the level of whole galaxies where stars and planets are born out of
rotating clouds of dust, so as to turn back again into clouds sooner
or later. We can also see that the Earth, and we together with it, is
made up of the dust of those distant worlds that at one time or
another exploded in outer space. When we think of that we can
well speak about the cosmic origin of life.

The circulation that we observe in outer space continues, by ex-
tension and on an immeasurably smaller scale, in our earthly conditions. For circulating on this tiny celestial body are the same elements as in the boundless universe.

When you and other scientists describe dispassionately the circulation of hydrogen and oxygen, nitrogen and carbon, sulfur and
phosphorus in nature, many nonspecialists are inclined to interpret
this as something that has nothing to do with them personally. Actually, all these things are part of the great whole, including our
short-lived earthly existence. For this is precisely how the entire
biosphere operates together with its complex communicative links
between organisms.

The soil that forms a thin layer around the skeleton of stone is
life, too, life from the past and life yet to be. Water constantly
circulates through the oceans, clouds, and rain, also through the
veins of foliage and through blood vessels. Atmospheric gases fill
all forms of life. Water, land, air, living organisms are constantly
exchanging all their components. The very idea that man, like any-

thing else on Earth, takes part in this gigantic circulation of matter fascinates me a lot more than ancient myths, however beautiful they may be.

A Y To say that man "takes part" is not accurate enough. Man's participation increasingly disrupts the circulations of matter and energy in the biosphere of the Earth. Very possibly we would not be here now discussing ecological problems if everything were all right with regard to these natural circulations. Something has happened in nature since the emergence of man. The circulation of matter, which had been well balanced until then, and which had, over billions of years, been changing at nature's bidding, suddenly broke into a gallop, spurred on by man on different sides.

The molecules that constituted the bodies of people were in their mass an infinitesimal part of the substance of the biosphere at the time man appeared on Earth. But over the last century the molecules, which are incorporated in human bodies, which make up our crops and the bodies of domesticated animals, the molecules, which owing to man's technogenic activity, had to change places, have formed such a mountain of substances that it has seriously disrupted, and sometimes even destroyed, some of the established streams of matter and energy in the biosphere. Sometimes it even creates new streams of matter and energy. Humankind has truly become a geological force. But this force often finds itself directed against the long-established mechanisms of the biosphere.

R E You are quite right. We would not be sitting here today and discussing these questions if it were not for one special episode in evolution.

When I spoke about the starting point I meant the dynamic balance in its natural state, when the "world police" Linné referred to held in check the various species that made up a great many forms of life.

Man cannot isolate himself from this circulation of which he is part. However, man differs from all the other creatures in that he is the only organism capable of consciously affecting this circulation.

This marked the turning point in the evolution of all living things on our planet. By increasing the propagation of his own species, by introducing numerous technical intricacies, and by consuming more and more resources of our planet, man has upset the balance and circulation that have taken shape over billions of years. Hence the dilemma: on the one hand man manipulates various ecosystems, replacing natural processes with his own, and on the other he cannot cut himself from the biosphere of which he is part. Every time he tries to do it, he does himself more harm than good.

There is one important feature that makes modern man different from his preindustrial predecessor. The latter maintained links with the rest of nature through pragmatic experiment and through his intuitive knowledge of it. He had neither the desire nor the ability to change his environment. If, postulating that life on Earth has existed for at least 3.5 billion years, we draw a line 3.5 meters long representing this period, the time that man has engaged in land cultivation would be equal to a mere one-hundredth of a millimeter. The time that has elapsed since the establishment of industrialism corresponds to one ten-millionth of a millimeter on the same scale. This can be seen only through a powerful microscope. However, it is precisely this period of time that man has changed and, indeed, spoiled the biosphere. We are especially concerned with the consequences because this process has come to its culminating point in our own time.

A Y There is a contradiction here. Being part of nature, man has split off from it, as it were. Nevertheless, as part of nature, we are subject to its laws. We grow and develop, eat and move, propagate and die in accordance with biological laws. As a creature that has separated from nature, man changes nature, he directs the actions of other living beings, and by breeding new animals and plants that did not exist before, he has learned to direct the evolution of living nature.

It turns out that as a creature segregated from nature, man has usurped the right, as it were, to order nature around. Are we really entitled to it? Or rather, are we ready to place ourselves at the head of nature and be its leader? It is true that man and humanity are the products of natural evolution. But are we perfect enough to assume responsibility for the nature around us? Our whole attitude to nature depends on how these questions are answered.

Meanwhile, as we look at our far from perfect human setup (imperfect from both political and technological points of view), we unwittingly come to the conclusion that our knowledge of ourselves is not sufficient, that we do not fully understand our place in nature.

RE I also think that we have no sufficient knowledge for that. Nevertheless, we have found ourselves in a position where we have to assume responsibility for further evolution on our planet. This responsibility requires that we, in spite of our far from exhaustive knowledge about various interrelationships, reconcile ourselves to the idea that, in the words of a philosopher, we are one of the notes in the great symphony of nature.

And this is where we go back to the remarkable, though dangerous, instrument you spoke about: the human brain. The brain became the main asset of the unprotected and vulnerable anthropoid ape in its struggle for existence, after it had come out of the shadows of the forest. All it had to rely on in order to survive was its inventiveness.

Once man came to realize the possibilities of his brain, he became confident of himself, indeed too much so. Enchanted by the new possibilities now open to him, he failed to see the delusions of his own mind. Until then man unconsciously accepted himself as an inalienable part of nature. But now he began to segregate himself from the rest of nature. The contradiction that had emerged between man and nature was both awkward and artificial. Man thus raised himself in rank to that of king of nature.

Jehovah blessed Noah and his sons with these words: "And the fear of you and the dread of you shall be upon every beast of the Earth, and upon every fowl of the air; with all wherewith the ground teemeth, and all the fishes of the sea, into your hand are they delivered."

It is impossible to articulate any better man's claim to domination. It would be a sheer folly to place the blame for this piece of arrogance upon religion—whether Christian, Judaic, or any other. All religious creeds have been created by man, and they reflect his own views of himself and his place in earthly existence.

This also applies to philosophical systems. Maybe you would like to say something about it?

A Y It might seem to an outsider that all these disquisitions have no direct bearing upon the subject. In actual fact, our behavior in the biosphere is the answer to the question of whether man is part of nature.

If man, according to the Old Testament, is the crowning achievement of creation and is therefore far removed from the rest of nature, then the laws of nature hold no sway over him, and we must actually be in command of nature. This is the way many people think. They also think that by his very essence man is a social being. This social concept of the essence of man directly leads to the technocratic interpretation of nature.

I think, and you will probably agree with me, that the following point of view is correct: man is only part of nature and will never be able to break away from it altogether, owing to the unity of physical and biological processes that determine both our own existence and the existence of all other living species in nature. In other words, the biosocial concept of man's essence and role is the only correct concept. We cannot command nature as we please; we should take biological laws into consideration!

Our attitude to nature is closely related to our different interpretations of the essence of man. If those who make decisions do not understand that man is a biosocial creature, their whole mentality becomes anti-ecological. Hence all the main global problems. I am sure the Christian concept of man being the crowning achievement of creation is at the back of the technocratic view of the world. Whether we like it or not, we will have to drift away from the Christian moral on this question and adopt an ecological moral if we want to keep the biosphere fit for the development of humankind. This new moral, or ecomoral, is a subject that deserves more detailed treatment.

Of course, there must be some sort of transitions between the two extreme (social and biosocial) points of view on the essence of man. I draw the dividing line between these approaches solely in order to better understand this problem.

RE Of course, we can say that both religious and philosophical systems prompt man to develop a view of himself as a social and not a biosocial creature. However, it would be more correct to say that man's religious creeds and myths have always taken shape in a given historical situation. When these creeds later turned into petrified dogmas they themselves affected the pattern of thinking and actions of subsequent generations.

When you speak of man as a biosocial creature that regards itself as a purely social creature, I recall Socrates's words in *Phaedrus* in reply to a rebuke that he did not understand nature sufficiently well: "You must forgive me, dear friend, I'm a lover of learning: trees and open country won't teach me anything, whereas men in the town do."

This is how many scholars and thinkers thought for hundreds of years. Thus the division of property between man and the rest of nature took root both in experimental science and in philosophy. We see this approach in "heretics" such as Galileo, in such a celebrated thinker as Descartes, and in such a great transformer of nature as Newton. It was necessary to study nature in order to fathom its laws. But at the same time nature existed as an object of utilization by man.

I don't think I will make a mistake saying that this dualism assumed a particularly fateful meaning when natural science and technology contracted a marriage of convenience. Man's faith that he has power over everything in this world has laid the ground for technology that is indifferent to nature. We have lost the ability to take life kindheartedly. And another thing: we have no respect any more for oneness, wholeness, the unimpaired state of things. And respect is precisely what we need in order to live on Earth according to its laws. We've created a robot that orders us around.

There is also a feedback connection. Technology is the product of the human brain. But subsequently technology leaves its own imprint on man and his activities. We have created a robot, and now the robot has subjected us to its will.

It seems to me that our brain has lured us onto the wrong track, which we continue to follow, as if no Darwins and no modern sciences—astrophysics, physics of elementary particles, and biology—have ever opened new horizons for us. But it is precisely these sciences and their achievements that could take us off the peaks of arrogance.

A Y In winding up our discussion about the nature of man I would like to summarize briefly. From the purely philosophical point of view man is the part of nature that is aware of its own existence. But how is it possible to determine the extent to which a dolphin or an ape is aware of its existence? For these are also levels (and high levels at that) of nature's self-awareness. We do not know this and it looks as if we are not going to for a long time. Any person who has spent several hours watching a band of apes would be surprised to see how similar this band is to human society. They have everything—love, jealousy, greed, aggressiveness, and friendship. There is no human quality that the apes do not have.

The longer we study living nature, the more "human" qualities (the qualities that we have always regarded as man's own prerogative) we see in living nature.

As a biologist I shall cite just one concrete example from my laboratory. We wanted to know how rats differ from one another when they are at the head of small groups. It is well known that in a small group they immediately form a hierarchy in which one animal stands at the head, and the others become subordinate to their leaders, while still others behave like those downtrodden and oppressed by all the other rats. The science of animal behavior has developed special tests that can tell which of the animals is intelligent and which, putting it bluntly, is stupid. Actually, these tests are not for gauging intelligence in general, but elementary rational activity. No tests for measuring stupidity have yet been discovered.

The tests we use are for determining the ability of a given animal to extrapolate. Using this criterion we learned how to find out the level of elementary rational activity for the leaders (so-called alpha-males), their "first deputies" (beta-males), and subordinates. It turned out that the leaders include both intelligent and stupid animals. The same holds true for subordinates, because there are both intelligent and stupid specimens among them. There are no statistical distinctions for intelligence among the groups of leaders and subordinates. Significantly, no fools were found among the "deputies." This raises a legitimate question: what are the makings of the leaders? There is only one answer: aggressiveness!

I am far from trying to extend the typical features of behavior of the rat community to human society. But come to think of it, Rolf, there must be something very similar between our society and the community of rats.

RE Of course, there is plenty of similarity (even a nonspecialist can tell that) between rats and men.

I am quite convinced that we can learn a great deal about ourselves by studying other species and their behavior. Such study is absolutely necessary if we ever hope to find an answer to the question of how we have found ourselves in our present state. We are confronted with a paradox. On the one side, using the potential of our brain, we have drifted away from the rest of nature, while on the other, we have inherited certain behavioral features from our biological past. Most likely we should look for the root of all our problems at this point of collision between the active new cortex of the brain and our behavior that we have inherited from primeval times.

Many different species exhibit everywhere a desire to have their own territory and show a high degree of aggressiveness in defending it against intruders, even if this aggressiveness is confined to a few demonstrative gestures. Territorial instinct, and the territorial imperative, are characteristic of all living things as an exhibition of the primeval instinct of preservation and continuation of life and its procreation. Territory provides food and in this way ensures the survival of the said species and its individual specimens.

Different species have different rules of ethics. Antelopes, for example, although they may come from different territories, meet at watering places; seals that jealously guard their territory on coastal rocks have passageways that they use in common. The birds that chirp their never-ending "don't invade my country" can have places where they obtain worms and seeds together. As for the territory itself, it is sacred.

Anthropologists can cite lots of examples of the existence of territorial instinct in pre-industrial communities. This instinct may be preserved in the existing groups of "living relics." The biologically defenseless man, who has no fangs, claws, or horns, found protection not only in his resourcefulness but also in the cohesion of the human race. The communal instinct afforded man protection, while the territory was guarded by the community. Thus the group defended the individual, and the latter defended the group. The members of the community developed what we call solidarity, based on the strongest possible foundation—personal interest.

With time, the communities grew into tribes, tribes into nations, and nations into alliances. They never lost the territorial instinct, but their territory grew wider and wider. Whether nationalism or patriotism, the words "right or wrong, this is my country" stand for the same primeval territorial instinct that once became part of the existing pattern of natural selection.

The powerful brain developed more weapons, making them more and more deadly. And when the same hand that once clutched the stick now holds the nuclear bomb, when the planet has become so small and so much better known to us than ever before, while man's ability to destroy has become universal, the territorial instinct which in the remote past assured the survival of a small band of people has turned into a deadly threat to the survival of the entire human species.

To my mind there is only one way out: the planet should be viewed as our common territory in the universe.

A Y I quite agree with your last conclusion, but I don't agree with your line of reasoning. I don't think that the feelings of patriotism for one's homeland should be reduced to the territorial instinct alone.

As I said, I recently visited a small island in the Pacific. There were only four scientists on that island, not counting several tens of thousands of seals, and possibly several million large mollusks-haliotis or abalones that we saw here and there on wet rocks above the water.

We studied the seals. The animals fought among themselves, played and behaved in many other ways to show that they were ready to protect their territory, as you said. They also had passageways which enabled the seals of different territorial communities to get to and from the sea. The rocks were covered with mollusks the size of your palm. But as it turned out (which was quite unexpected for me, although mollusk specialists knew that long ago) these seemingly immobile creatures often fight among themselves. And how! If you look at a section of the rock where haliotis made their home for any length of time, you will notice that some of them—very slowly and even imperceptibly—close in on their neighbors, sharply increase the speed of their progress and then knock their shells against the shells of the other mollusks, trying push them off the rock. I would not have believed that if I had not seen it all with my own eyes. But at first glance the haliotis look almost completely immobile, as if they were part of that rock.

Apparently, the reason for this territorial instinct in the mollusks is a natural desire to get more food: if there are too many mollusks sitting on one rock, each one of them will have less food. The territorial instinct will not directly develop into a social instinct. What actually happens is the other way around: it will ensure a broader distribution of mollusks wherever they could make their home.

Having emerged out of living nature, man has eventually become a biosocial creature. We cannot reduce all our specific features either to biology or to sociology: our whole behavior and our whole life come out of complex combinations of all these biological and social elements.

We must always remember that we do not know more than we

do, and so it will always be. On the face of it this pessimistic conclusion inevitably comes out of another precept, namely, that the process of cognition has no limit and that each new discovery raises more questions than it answers. You are right, saying that over the past several centuries something very serious has happened. Humanity, with its territorial division among tribes and nations, the national boundaries that have criss-crossed the surface of our planet, reached an ecological dead end.

No state in the world can solve global ecological problems by itself. However, these problems must be solved. Our globe has become too small in the light of our technical achievements, and humanity has fewer and fewer possibilities to manifest the traditional territoriality.

RE The territorial imperative of seals and mollusks that you observed is in a way their nationalism and patriotism, as it were.

But let's not play around with semantics. We understand that the Earth is too small to stay divided into territories disputed by different countries. Let's face it. What was good for a band of men and a tribe has become a grave threat to the entire human species.

To ward off this threat we need what you have mentioned before: respect that is at the root of ecological morality.

We shall return to this somewhat later.

DAY

6

THE TECHNOCRATS ARE TRYING TO CONVINCE
US THAT THE PROBABILITY OF MAJOR
ACCIDENTS ... IS NEGLIGIBLE. BUT THE LESS
LIKELY A MAJOR INDUSTRIAL ACCIDENT THE
LESS WE ARE PREPARED FOR IT, AND THE MORE
TERRIBLE ITS CONSEQUENCES, SHOULD ONE
HAPPEN! CHERNOBYL AND BHOPAL ARE
VIVID PROOF OF THAT.

—ALEXEI YABLOKOV

THE MORE COMPLEX THE TECHNICAL AND
SOCIAL STRUCTURE OF SOCIETY IS, THE MORE
THERE ARE ANONYMOUS EXPERTS CROWDING
INTO THE CORRIDORS OF POWER. THE ACTUAL
DECISIONS ARE OFTEN SHAPED BY THE
INVISIBLE BUREAUCRACY.

—ROLF EDBERG

■

AY When we spoke about the future of man and nature we started our conversation with a nuclear Armageddon. We also spoke about the global problems facing humankind, and what we must do in order to be able to advance rapidly and not lead a piteous existence in the wake of the deteriorating conditions on our planet. This is why we devoted the whole of the fifth day of our dialogue to the essence of man's life. Let's now look at man from a somewhat different angle, or rather at the artificial environment and technology (machinery, industry, production, and so forth) that man has created and surrounded himself with.

Every one of us and society as a whole have long since broken away from our initial natural surroundings, and have done so with the help of technology, which, in turn, is the source of all evil for the biosphere. However, it is technology that is the hope for changing the situation for the better, although nobody can predict how technology will develop. What is your opinion? Do you think technology will help solve global problems?

RE I think it can, but only partially and under certain conditions. In the first place, a lot depends on the historical perspective in which we view ourselves and our actions. I think that our worries and our panic are largely the result of our inability to look far ahead. What we should do is to look back to the remote past in order to understand what is happening today and why. Why is it, for example, that we have drifted away from a life of harmony with nature and have gradually created an increasingly artificial environment? We talked about it yesterday, but we must also try and look as far into the future as possible in order to inscribe ourselves and the surging events around us into a wider context.

Looking back over the years we can see how rapid industrial progress has brought us into the present-day technological world. The same hand that ten thousand years ago held stone tools now directs space probes on their way to the frontiers of the solar system. Technology has made ours a small world. Magellan's *Victoria* took three years to circumnavigate the world. Phileas Fogg in Jules Verne's famous novel completed the job in eighty days. Today manned and unmanned satellites circle our whole planet within ninety minutes.

The Earth is integrated now in a giant network of technological dependencies. The entire trend is toward technological unification, so that wherever you go you will see the same cars, the same fuel for their engines, the same hard-surfaced roads, the same high-rises, the same television sets, clothing, power saws, and excavating machinery. We have created one global technological civilization, which is the product of our century. Actually Western-style technology has spread throughout the world.

Speaking of civilization, I have in mind cooperation between people in the utilization of existing technology and in its further development. In this light I would sum up the culture of our civilization as a bank of judgments of people and a bank of the rules of their behavior.

A Y   In other words, you are viewing civilization and culture as two different things.

R E   Yes. It is true that technological civilization has brought about standardization. But at the same time we have numerous different cultures, each one of which rests on its own tradition. But when these traditions break down (and there are many examples of this), the result is the loss of the traditional roots and alienation.

I believe that one of our main tasks is to unite global technological civilization with local cultures that make the world richer and more varied, and in a way, more secure.

But there is the other side of the problem. Technological progress has strengthened international dependence, whereas national states, many of which took their present shape back in the days of the sailing ship and the steam engine, have since consolidated and become unwieldy and cumbersome as their sphere of influence has expanded. The conflict between these two trends—technological globalism and the ever more ponderous state machinery—poses what are probably the greatest threats to our future. To my mind this is a crucial problem, which I do not know how to resolve.

A Y   In its present shape technology gives more trouble than hope for solving ecological problems. This is why I take the whole idea of expanding modern technologies with a grain of salt, in spite of the fact that, as a member of human society, I am constantly making use of them. I think 90 percent of all new technologies have a destructive effect on nature. New technologies are spreading throughout the world at frightening speed, and these enable us to bring still greater pressure to bear on nature. It is true that the concerted efforts of all countries to expand and make fuller use of new technologies lead to unpredictable and at times catastrophic results for nature.

Not long ago the world experienced a fuel crisis. In one way or another this crisis affected all countries. Aside from its socioeconomic roots, the crisis led to intensification of the ecologically dangerous exploitation of oil deposits on the oceanic shelf, in the tundra and arboreal zones of Eurasia and North America and also to a situation where 15 percent of the surface of the World Ocean was covered with an oil film. One of the principal reasons for this crisis was the utilization of similar or identical technologies in different countries.

We spoke about the catastrophic destruction of the tropical rain forests. This expanding process has become possible owing to the growing utilization of efficient technologies.

Of course, progress cannot be stopped, and technology will continue to develop. However, we can already see that if we do not render our technologies more ecological, the very development of technology alone will turn into another global problem like many others that we have discussed and which, incidentally, have largely been brought about by application of new technologies.

The only practical way out of this situation is the creation and expansion of such technologies that would support the natural environment rather than destroy it. So far, the development of technology has proceeded chaotically with a view to quick results and the pursuance of political (or rather military) objectives.

The state of the biosphere calls for ecological criteria whereby new technologies are developed. We need technologies for recycling materials that have already been obtained from nature. Also technologies that would consume natural resources more sparingly on things that we can well do without. We know that modern transport facilities make people a lot more mobile than ever before. But is it all that necessary always to move from place to place? From the point of view of more rational use of natural resources, would it not be more expedient, instead of assembling people at one place for conferences or congresses, to ensure their communication by way of television facilities so they could discuss important issues without actually traveling over long distances? I spoke about it at one of our previous sessions.

Modern technology has led to a situation in which the face of our Earth has become furrowed by motorways, their number increasing at a terrifying rate. Would it not be more expedient to develop underground public transport between large cities without disturbing the natural environment so it can continue to function and support human life?

I think the time has come to revise our previous priorities of technological progress. What would you say to that?

R E You are right. Technological civilization has two sides: a good side and a bad side. By the bad side I mean the large-scale disruption of nature. Taken by itself, technology is neutral, for we decide whether it should be used for creative or destructive purposes.

You went to the very heart of the matter when you mentioned the terrifying rate of technological development. On the face of it, high technology, with its data banks and other information facilities, is necessary to ease our problems with an eye to the future, which I spoke about. For some reason, however, we misuse our opportunities. One Swedish industrialist aptly noted that we use technical facilities in order to circulate around the Earth even faster, to step up the tempo of this circulation and make purblind decisions. The philosopher Georg von Wright said that industrial technology would continue its "mad dance in bacchanal inebriation" by further polluting and despoiling the natural environment and would in this way bring us closer and closer to the day of retribution. We must come to our senses and clearly outline the tasks of our technology.

You've spoken about modern communication facilities, television among them. This I think is an excellent example of how technology can be used for good and evil purposes.

Exceptionally positive is the fact that television, more than anything else, has in our time, shortened the distance between nations. Every one of us can, without actually leaving his armchair, see the natural zones of our planet, learn about their beauty and about the fantastic wealth of life forms. Dag Hammarskjöld once spoke about the speed at which the signals are sent through nerves from an open wound to all parts of the organism of humanity. Such signals can also be transmitted by television. We see the exodus of people from areas afflicted by famine and war, we see black demonstrators in Pretoria being attacked by the police armed with truncheons and automatic weapons. Very often we follow events at the very moment they are taking place. We can see and hear those who are in control of the destinies of the world, with Mikhail Gorbachev and Ronald Reagan on our television screens in front of us.

At the same time television, which has put us in contact with the whole wide world, has also opened the floodgates for stultifying and brutalizing influences. People have become the victims of spiritual and intellectual pollution that put our cultural traditions at risk. I think that here we should be on our guard.

Young people often spend four and even five hours in front of the box. This gives many researchers grounds to believe that society may soon be overwhelmed by a new type of illiteracy. As we know words are formed by the tongue and the lips. In earlier times an illiterate person was one who could not read. But now we are threatened by still more primitive illiteracy: the inability to formulate phrases expressing our thoughts and feelings.

And yet I believe that we should appreciate this new and wonderful feeling of interdependence brought to us by this new mass medium. Thoughts and ideas that used to take decades to bring to the knowledge of others are now disseminated throughout the world with lightning speed.

Television can also be an irreplaceable means of diffusion of ecological knowledge and an effective instrument for live perception of the natural environment.

A Y You are quite right that there are no "bad technologies" as such. The great danger to nature and society comes from utilization of certain specific technologies.

I agree that television is among the most developed technologies in society. But the same technology can be used for good and evil purposes.

One and the same fact can be shown on the television screen. Yet it can be commented on in different ways thus having a different effect on public opinion. Whether accidentally or by design, he who shapes the contents of television broadcasts also shapes the ideology of the viewers. Technologically we can at any moment be present at any point on Earth and receive the latest news within seconds, and yet we may at the same time be ill-informed. If we see only part of the truth, then the viewer will be misinformed rather than informed. Being technically perfect, television is far from being morally or ethically perfect.

What should then be done in order to put television at the service of good only, and not at the service of evil? Nobody can ban television. It seems to me that the way out is to develop television still further. To make my point clear I shall draw an analogy with books. There are many different books at a library: about nature and about history, novels and poetry, detective stories, books about crimes and instruments of torture, also pornography—all of which give the full spectrum of human culture. But most people look in these books not for prescriptions for poison, but for something good. Society is developing under the influence of well-prepared books with a pronounced humanistic slant, and not books like *Mein Kampf*. Maybe television should have 110 channels, and not 2 or even 10?

Television may not be a very good example of how modern technology affects the way we utilize our natural resources. But modern technology is fraught with dangers stemming from its very substance, the dangers which we did not dwell on in our discussion. What I have in mind is the ecological risk which stems from the development of new technologies. For example, television transmitting stations, and even television sets at home are the sources of microwave radiation that are far from being absolutely safe for all living creatures, including you and me.

This is a constant danger, so to speak. And what about the ecological risk linked with industrial accidents? A major industrial accident may lead to consequences that can be compared only to the consequences of nuclear war. It is very indicative, for example, that to satisfy the needs of the power industry alone about ten billion tons of equivalent fuel are extracted, transported, stored, and used in just one year. And all that does not include gasoline for cars, or fuel for ships and airplanes. We can say that the amount of fuel capable of burning and exploding contains as much energy (or possibly more) as the entire arsenal of nuclear weapons. From the point of view of both ecology and security for man and nature, this is a tremendous latent danger. The same could be said about many conventional industrial products such as ammonium, arsenic, phosgene, barium, and prussic and other acids. Every year hundreds of billions and even trillions of lethal doses of these substances are processed and stored. Their total lethal effect is one or two orders of magnitude higher than all the existing radioactive substances.

The technocrats are trying to convince us that the probability of major accidents at atomic power stations, at chemical plants, and at other similar establishments dangerous to man and nature is negligible. But the less likely a major industrial accident, the more terrible are its consequences, should one happen! Chernobyl and Bhopal are vivid proof of that.

We have learned to live together with the tremendous and ever increasing risks of modern technology and somehow are not conscious of it in our day-to-day routine. This means that we have slowly eased into an ecologically dangerous global situation.

RE It is clear that television should be more widely used for the good of society. However, formal freedom of choice does not guarantee that it will serve the good of society whether the television set has ten channels or a hundred. Propaganda pressure can affect anyone's choice.

I shall come back to this question in a different connection. But now I would like to touch upon other things in order to show the difficulties that the individual encounters in modern society.

I shall start out with the political apparatus. The more complex the technical and social structure of society is, the more there are anonymous experts crowding into the corridors of power. The actual decisions are often shaped by the invisible bureaucracy which, acting over the heads of citizens, affects all the many things that concern their everyday life and their well-being. In large states there is a great danger that the seemingly democratic decision-making process is acquiring formalistic features.

I am talking about the countries of the West. I believe that in the Soviet Union its citizens traditionally have a limited access to information.

Another question that often puts me to thinking is this: could the new high-tech society be getting increasingly weighted down with class contradictions that even the most far-sighted thinkers of the nineteenth century were unable to foresee? Isn't there a risk of a heavily computerized society developing a class rift between those who are in charge of technology and information, on the one hand, and those who are controlled by the ruling apparatus, on the other?

Already the economy and the mass media are almost entirely in the hands of vested interest groups. Earlier on I spoke about the role of propaganda in controlling and manipulating people. The obtrusive propaganda (advertising, if you like) of "fashionable" products makes people dissatisfied with what they already have and induces them to buy new things, even though this so-called "novelty" boils down to insignificant exterior alterations. So these commodities grow obsolete even before they get worn out physically, which leads to wasting the resources of our planet.

As for new technical projects it is important that society study them well in advance and reject those that could have serious uncontrollable consequences. Just like you, Alexei, I also consider that in the future the ecological principle must be the basis of all new technical innovations and projects. Our present dilemma comes from the lack of wisdom in the application of our knowledge.

There are many things that are possible, but not everything is useful and by far not everything is necessary. There are many projects that we would do well to drop altogether, either because we know their possible effects very well or because we know too little about them. The effects of rapidly developing technology are often so great that any mistake can easily provoke a critical situation. This is why, to my mind, it is so important to take a long view of everything we do.

A Y Neither of us is expert at technology. Rather we are consumers of this technology. As I can see, today both you and I look at technology and its development somewhat apprehensively and always from the angle of the relationship between man and nature.

It looks like any new technology raises the same problems everywhere: it must be held up for ecological scrutiny. In my country we have been trying—albeit not very successfully—to have any new material and product, also any new industrial project, examined by state commissions of ecological experts. However, the development of technologies proceeds at a faster pace. Here is an example. A large part of my country is taken up by the tundra and forest-tundra. These areas have valuable reserves of mineral deposits and other natural wealth. By tradition these resources are prospected with the help of powerful cross-country vehicles. Today all of our tundra is literally scarred with furrows left by these vehicles. As it has turned out, the lichen growing in the tundra are very vulnerable to such treatment. After even one trip made by a caterpillar vehicle, this cover is practically destroyed and stays that way for whole decades. Now we should admit that the utilization of modern machinery in the tundra is anti-ecological.

If we had come to this conclusion thirty years ago we could have switched to hovercraft and we would have demanded a total ban on the use of caterpillar vehicles in the tundra already in use at that time. This is just one example of what an ecologically incompetent and shortsighted practice can do.

In any event, the transition from technocratic to ecological technology is inevitable, if we want to save the nature of the Earth. Of course, this transition is going to be both slow and painful. And here again we come up against the problem we talked about yesterday: has man hived off from nature or is he part of nature? And this question: is man a social or a biosocial being? With the present consensus that man is a social being, technocratic snobbishness and the anti-ecological attitude to any technology will prevail.

RE You are talking about ecological technology. This is what many people, including you and me, have been referring to as very essential.

Some enthusiasts want to take us back to the old modes of production and consumption. This is an exercise in futility. We cannot throw away the knowledge we have acquired. Nor can we improve and perfect this world without technology.

What we do need are new technologies. We need this not only for correcting old mistakes, but (which is even more important) also for warding off new and probably still worse mistakes.

The global environmental problems brought forth by technocratic thinking have turned us into citizens of the World Polluted States. Therefore, to solve these problems, it is necessary to have well organized international cooperation. Not a single nation, and not a single person can be viewed as some sort of island in the ocean. All of us are linked by common earthly concerns, and this is why we are all dependent on one another.

I am convinced that the most important problem now is to satisfy the essential needs of people. Poverty and famine dehumanize man. We cannot take it lying down when large groups of people live in humiliating poverty. Before anything else, we must assure a satisfactory material standard of living for the poorest. What I have in mind is human solidarity, the responsibility of the industrially developed countries for social groups that have not got enough economic strength.

And this is where we again unavoidably come to a question that looms large in our dialogue, the question of the need to promote solidarity with the people of the future. The rich countries, regardless of their political systems, are lacking in global responsibility, in the understanding of the need for economic planning that would serve the interests of the entire planet.

In spite of all the alarming signals, many officials in a decision-making capacity, whatever the political system they represent, have insufficient knowledge of ecology. We are shocked to hear that nine-tenths of the population in some country cannot read or write. But the ecological illiteracy of many people at many levels is just as great, and this illiteracy is fraught with much greater danger for humankind.

In a varying degree ecological illiteracy exists everywhere. However, an observer from a small country has the impression that this illiteracy is particularly great in large and strong countries that are chiefly responsible for our common future.

Please tell me, Alexei, what should be done so that the powers-that-be embrace greater global responsibility for and understanding of ecological imperatives?

A Y This is a good question. I would say that this question concerns not only ecological illiteracy, but also the anti-ecological approach in general. It is hard to say that the leaders of the World Bank are ecologically illiterate. This bank has billions of dollars; it maintains a staff of thousands of experts who can quickly solve any problem.

The bank's directors can have any information, they can instantly receive answers to practically any ecological question. Nevertheless the World Bank finances the destruction of the tropical forests in different parts of the world. Thus it commits one of the most terrible ecological crimes among the many others that are being perpetrated in the world today.

And all that affair with Lake Baikal, when one-fourth of the world's fresh water reserves is threatened with industrial pollution as a result of the departmental ambitions of the Ministry of Pulp and Paper Industry alone!

This means that the anti-ecological practices may not only be the product of ecological illiteracy, but may be intentional, the result of deliberate actions.

In the West anti-ecological decisions are prompted by quick returns. In my country they are justified by the need of government departments to report the fulfillment of a plan. Ecologically versed managers who make anti-ecological decisions could well be called ecological adventurers. Whatever reasons may be provided for justifying this ecological adventurism, it becomes extremely dangerous for society and for civilization in general. The ecological adventurism exhibited by ecologically educated people (or those who have access to ecological advice) can be summed up in one word—immoral.

RE What you say shows up the dangers that surround us. Regrettably, we do not give them much thought. To see these dangers we must be keenly aware of what is going on. As it is, we encounter more and more problems to which we cannot always find a ready answer.

Some of these problems are associated with the use of high technology. How do the increasingly more powerful magnetic and electric fields around the globe affect man? We have already spoken about computers. And this is just another problem: computers are becoming a customary part of our daily routine, like wrist-watches, like the telephone and the car. I wonder if there will be any room left in our heavily computerized world for human feelings and considerations?

A Y These are increasingly important problems, as they boil down to the attitude of the individuals to political, technocratic, and economic power.

R E I would like to touch upon genetic engineering, which is a relatively new science. It looks as if over the past several decades biological science has been developing faster than physics and other exact sciences, in spite of the progress made by physics of elementary particles. At the same time the borderline between biology and physics is disappearing. There is no such point where we would stop and say: here inanimate matter comes to an end and biological life begins.

Very possibly it is at the junction of biology and physics that a new picture of the world appears, one that may leave its imprint on the whole of the next century.

Yet, the pace of technological development is as worrying as it is nebulous at least to a nonexpert. As we penetrated the fathomless depths of matter we brought to life the cosmic powers encapsulated in nuclear energy, with all its countless dangers. This discovery raised another problem: when we penetrate deeper into the cell and into the heredity code, what good will that do us, and what is there on the negative side, considering the possible danger of this penetration? It looks as if we have opened a new field full of great possibilities and great hazards.

An odd situation is shaping up: at first the chemists poison farm fields and life on Earth and after that genetic engineers invade the cell in order to correct the results of this massive contamination.

Just as the laser beam can cure and destroy, here, too, genetic engineering can play a dual role. On the one hand, it plays the positive role in combating disease and helping in the selection of farm crops in order to feed more people. On the other hand, any manipulation with human heredity is fraught with danger. And this, in turn, raises important ethical problems.

What would you, Alexei, say, as a biologist, to a concerned nonspecialist about this?

A Y You are not the only one who worries about the consequences of genetic engineering. I think that in this case, like in the case of nuclear energy, man has touched upon the fundamentals of his being, and has gone so deep into matter that the very idea of it boggles the mind of the layman. Besides, the layman simply does not have sufficient knowledge to foresee all the long-term effects of this intrusion.

What is actually happening? A detailed knowledge of the genetic code has equipped biologists to build new parts into the hereditary molecules. This is what it looks like schematically. Biologists first find organisms that have certain useful properties, such as frost resistance. After that they try to separate out the genes that are responsible for building up frost resistance and then insert these genes into other organisms, such as strawberries, for example. The result is a new plant which thus acquires the ability to grow within a wider range of temperatures.

Or another example. As is known, some plants produce chemical substances that repel harmful insects. A successful attempt was made to separate out a gene which synthesizes an insect repellent, and to include this gene into the organism of different plants which, for some time at least, become protected from (meaning simply not tasty to) the attacking insects.

Work is said to have been going on to make plants "self-fertilizing." These works proceed from the fact that leguminous plants are able to fix nitrogen from the air by way of tubercular bacteria living on their roots. This is why leguminous plants enrich the soil with nitrogen. An attempt has been made to include into the genetic apparatus of maize and some other cultivated plants certain genes that would make it possible to create a similar symbiosis with nitrogen-fixing bacteria of plants from other phyla. This may possibly be done in the future.

However, all such attempts that are at first glance extremely useful and necessary do not provide the answer to your question. We do not know all the consequences of such intervention in the holy of holies of life itself—the mechanism that governs heredity. So far only the genom (a set of genes) of the simplest organisms, like those of certain bacteria, has been studied. Their genom is thousands and even tens of thousands of times as simple as that of higher organisms. Work is under way on the international project for decoding the genetic human code. If we succeed in switching on to this job all the leading laboratories in the field of molecular biology in the world and pool the money that totals in the billions rather than millions of dollars, then, according to very conservative estimates, we shall solve the mystery of our genetic code in twenty or thirty years. This shows the scale and complexity of the job. It is clear, though, that in this extremely complicated structure nothing can be altered without seriously affecting the rest of it.

As I see it, genetic engineers are not yet trying to find out what else, in addition to the frost resistance or taste of the leaves, has changed in organisms into which alien genes have been planted. Any organism is not a mere mosaic made up of independent parts, but a complex interrelated system. Alongside getting a practical effect, what we want to achieve, we are sure to alter something that we have not bargained for and, as a result, we get some unpredictable and, as a rule, negative effects of our invasion of the genetic code.

Therefore let's not place great hopes on genetic engineering, for it can at best be a method of obtaining material for subsequent painstaking selection, in the process of which the genom unbalanced by our intrusion will regain its stability.

Ecological engineering is another matter. It is spoken of much less often than genetic engineering. I shall cite an example to explain what it is all about. The mass killing of cackling geese at their wintering places in Turkey reduced their population in the Swedish tundra from 30,000 in 1953 to two to three hundred specimens in 1983. To save the dying population, the eggs of some of these birds were placed into the nests of barnacle geese whose population in Sweden is very large. Barnacle geese spend their winter in relatively secure areas in Holland and some other countries of Western Europe. Thus the cackling geese hatched out in the nests of their adoptive parents and, together with them, flew to their wintering places in western Europe and not in Turkey. I have heard that now a whole new population of cackling geese has been created, and these have for several years been wintering at new places. I call this ecological engineering. This, of course, raises rather complex questions (such as the transport of parasites to regions where they generally do not live). However, such questions can be dealt with, using the knowledge at our disposal. I think ecological engineering holds out great promise for the future.

RE But this sort of activity calls for extensive knowledge, constructive imagination, and moral integrity. Are you sure people who have acquired this new power will always have these three qualities?

AY Even this short exchange of views about the links between modern technology and ecology suggests rather pessimistic conclusions. The rich countries, which have information, knowledge, and money, often act anti-ecologically. We have already cited many examples of such anti-ecological practices. The attempts of the world community somehow to change the situation are not very effective. Back in 1972, the United Nations, aware of the pressing need to solve ecological problems, created a special agency called UNEP. The actual state of affairs had hardly been changed seriously. The UN and some individual countries have made many fine decisions on nature conservation, but the results are inadequate. Does this mean that all our efforts are in vain, that we are losing out, and that it is impossible to organize a reasonable management of nature at present?

Although the ecological situation remains serious and at times plain tragic, we must not give up on that. Things are not as bad as they seem sometimes. And there are also reasons for cautious optimism.

For instance, the worldwide green movement is growing and this is something we must reckon with. Pollution of the World Ocean continues on a wide scale, but the rate of expansion of such pollution has markedly gone down. The number of protected zones and their total area are growing. Some twenty years ago a mere 0.5 percent of the territory of the Earth was under such protection, whereas now nature protection zones, nature preserves, and national parks take up some 2 to 3 percent. If this tendency continues, the protected area will then grow to 5 percent by the year 2000. This, of course, is far from sufficient for maintaining biological variety and for preserving the principal ecosystems. But the very fact that this tendency exists, that it is developing in a very important direction is very encouraging.

There are many examples of how man has succeeded in saving some almost extinct biological species. In 1920 there were about 700 European beavers in the Soviet Union. Today their population has grown to as many as 250,000. In the 1920s we had only a few thousand sable, whereas now their population of hundreds of thousands is open to hunting. Some sixty years ago there were a mere fifteen hundred to two thousand saiga (steppe antelopes) in the USSR. Today there are more than two million of them. Fifty years ago the population of European bison was only thirty, whereas now there are more than two thousand of them on the continent. There are many such examples in Europe and North America, which proves that man can preserve wildlife!

In many countries special genetic banks—storage of genetic material such as seeds, embryos, cell cultures and sperm—are being set up. This is a very expensive business, the same as the conversion of zoos into centers for conservation and propagation of rare species (today dozens of species of vertebrates live only in captivity). However, a mere comparison between the money necessary for this job and the money being spent on armament shows that society has the necessary resources.

The main problem is that the influential decision-making groups need to adopt an ecological way of thinking. Some encouraging moves have already been made in this direction. In most countries all political parties, without exception, are beginning to include ecological demands in their platforms. Statesmen with high ecological motivations are elected to top government posts in some countries, such as Mexico, Tanzania, Norway, Sweden, and Australia.

In all probability, humankind can develop on Earth and can resolve the ecological crisis it has precipitated. But to achieve this, it is important to change the prevailing moral climate in society. The ecological imperative must become a moral imperative. But how can society develop an ecological morality? This is a very important (possibly the most crucial) question.

RE I am glad to hear the examples you just cited showing that it is possible to achieve practical results in the struggle for a better natural environment. We had to give lots of grim examples since we wanted to paint a realistic picture of the present situation. It is necessary to see evil in order to fight it. But, of course, lots of positive things are being done, too, and that, I think, should encourage us to new efforts.

Your list of such examples could be made much longer, of course. All we have to do is to go a quarter of a century back in order to see how rapidly the environmental protection movement has grown. The anxiety and vigilance of broad sections of the population guarantee that the ecological crisis will eventually be overcome.

A poll run among constituents in my country showed that of all the political questions the most important of all was that of the natural environment. You must have noticed that the political parties of different countries include this problem in their platforms; they feel the pressure of public opinion. Many governments have set up ministries for nature conservation, as well as other state agencies concerned with ecological questions. Incidentally, the organization that you represent has set up cooperation with our nature protection agencies. After the Stockholm conference of 1972 the environmental agency under the auspices of the United Nations was set up. Regrettably, this organization has not yet been promoted to the status of all the other UN specialized agencies.

In many places initial environment purification is done, which has a particularly noticeable effect in lakes. I have already spoken about the outrageous dumping and burning of waste material in the North Sea. Now there are encouraging signs that in several years this practice will be abandoned. It has been proved that when the authorities introduce stringent laws and rules, new purification methods are introduced, although previously they were thought unfeasible. In some countries products are marked with a special stamp. Farming methods that do not use chemicals are encouraged, too. In Sweden many scientists, conservationists, and even concerned groups of schoolchildren have mounted an extensive and successful campaign, now internationally known, against the chloride bleaching of paper which leaves poisonous residue on paper diapers, napkins, milk containers, and notebooks.

A great deal has been and is being done in this respect. However, the more impatient of us think that the measures in question are much too limited and much too slow. You have noted yourself that the situation with the natural environment is not getting any better, but is in fact deteriorating. No sooner do you achieve success in one direction than you hear warning signals coming from other critical areas.

A Y You spoke about making use of the time we still have.

R E There is no justification for the loss of time in the arms race, which has consumed staggering material and human resources so vitally necessary for fighting poverty and protecting the environment. The time at our disposal is getting shorter with every passing year. We do not know when and where we shall reach the point of no return. There are such limits in every area of human endeavor. Once we pass this limit, ecological development may soon enter its crucial phase.

This is why I am convinced that it is not sufficient to make partial adjustments in the existing system of production. We fully concur in that we cannot do without technology. But modern industrial society, with its predatory approach to nature, with its prodigious waste of resources and its environmental contamination, with its cynical view of man as a creature that consumes and does not give anything in return, does not, to my mind, have a chance of survival. It looks as if industrialism, which we have seen developing over the past two hundred years in the East and in the West, has fulfilled its historic role and must now leave the stage.

This is the way many people think. Our optimism born of the initial successes of industrialism was followed by disappointment. Many young people are turning away from industrial civilization. More and more people are becoming increasingly aware of the dangers for the environment brought forth by our industrial society. We have clearly reached the stage when, in order to assure the survival of our own species, it is necessary to work out fundamentally new methods of production based on man's needs for a pollution-free environment, also for something that would lend more meaning and substance to his existence.

In all its numerous manifestations technology reflects a given social system. We are trying to feel out different ways to a society based on values and priorities different from those we now have.

I want to go back for a moment to what you said a little while ago: man can live on Earth, and we can curb the ecological crisis. But this calls for a society that has espoused an essentially ecological outlook. The way to such a society lies via a new morality.

Tomorrow we shall speak on this subject in greater detail.

AY The industrialism you mentioned is the same old technocratism that we have already talked about. Of course, it will not be done away with without battle. The technocrats will not surrender their positions without a fight. There is no doubt that all our hopes, or rather our main hope, rest with the youth. Our hopes are for the young people's common sense, for their natural desire to live on a prosperous planet, and not on a sick and degraded one.

Some time ago I was asked to speak before a conference of student groups for the protection of nature. When I was a university student thirty-five years ago there were two or three such groups of activists, but now they come in hundreds. They do a lot of good things—from fighting against poachers to promoting ecological education and grappling with practical problems such as purification of air and water. Their mottoes are wonderful: "If we don't do that, who will?" "When, if not now?" or "Tomorrow will be too late!"

DAY

7

TO MY SURPRISE, OUR POINTS OF VIEW EITHER
CONCURRED OR WERE VERY SIMILAR ON MOST
ISSUES. AND THIS GIVES ME THE IDEA THAT TO THE
READER OUR DIALOGUE MAY SOUND VERY
MUCH LIKE A DUET.
—ALEXEI YABLOKOV

I THINK THAT IF THE NUMBER OF SUCH
DIALOGUES ACROSS IDEOLOGICAL FRONTIERS
INCREASED, PEOPLE WOULD, TO THEIR GREAT
SURPRISE, SEE HOW MUCH THERE IS IN THIS
WORLD THAT BRINGS THEM CLOSER TOGETHER.
—ROLF EDBERG

A Y For a full six days we have been discussing the problem of man and nature. And every day we have said in one way or another that a new morality is sure to emerge. All that is quite clear, since morality is a system of views and philosophies that reflects our understanding of human existence. In other words, for each one of us and for society as a whole morality is defined as "what is good and what is bad." It is impossible to invent a morality. It arises out of the life of society, out of our existence, out of our attitude to one another, and out of man's attitude to nature.

I think that neither the Christian, nor the Buddhist, not any other morality in the way they were initially formulated encompasses all the complex problems of interrelation between man and nature, the problems that we now have to resolve. It seems we have come close to formatting a new morality which could be called "ecomorality," or "ecosophy," as you like to call it.

I cannot take it upon myself to formulate all aspects of ecomorality in our dialogue. It is for a scientist and philosopher to do this. Many books have been written about it, with many more to come. Nevertheless, I consider it my duty to raise some key provisions of ecomorality. But before we proceed to this, we should discuss some approaches to this new morality or rather name the problems that still have to be solved.

The first such problem is moral degradation that inevitably arises from technological development. This is what Descartes said, as well as the French philosophers of the age of Enlightenment, and Karl Marx himself. This is a very complex problem. The amorality of the technocrats can be judged not from the positions of some fossilized morality but from the positions of an emerging new morality. And it is from these positions that we should understand the postulate about the moral degradation of technocracy. The complexity of this problem also comes from the fact that as the moral degradation of the technocratic section of society deepens, the section of society that understands the futility of any technocratic solution to the problems of interrelationship between man and nature becomes more advanced in a moral sense.

The second problem comes from the fact that the role of living nature in the system of human values has changed markedly. I shall cite a few examples to make my point clear. A well-trained killer whale (a large dolphin) costs about one-and-a-half million dollars. The average price of human life in Sweden (life insurance) is about half a million dollars. A young gorilla costs about seventy thousand dollars, and a falcon in the middle East may cost forty-five thousand dollars. The gall bladder of a bear costs several thousand dollars, and a portion of roast made of the paws of this animal in a posh Japanese restaurant costs eight hundred dollars. The U.S. Congress earmarked twenty-five million dollars for saving the California condor: one million dollars for each bird. And what is the price of the life of one of those forty million people who die of famine every year? What is the price of the young soldiers who died in the war between Iran and Iraq, and in other political conflicts?

There are also other ways of determining the cost of a living creature. It is well known to ecologists that any ecosystem can function normally until an average of 10 percent of its elements has been disrupted. After that the ecosystem disintegrates and passes down to a lower information-and-energy level.

For example, Sweden's natural environment, which enables people to live and work in the country, is a uniform ecosystem made up of numerous living organisms and their habitat. If 10 percent of Sweden's plants, animals, fungi microorganisms, and so forth, disappear, the country will not be able to produce its gross national product. Knowing the size of Sweden's gross national product, we can say that one animal and plant species in this country costs about half a million dollars.

So it turns out that the cost of human life may be very low, while the cost of living nature for humanity may rise sharply. This tendency takes its most extreme form in the attempts to reduce the birth rate, as is the case in many countries. If society is compelled to deliberately reduce the rate of reproduction and refuse to allow the emergence of new lives, these unborn lives can, in a sense, be of negative value.

And finally, the third problem is the lesser dependence of every individual person on nature, in spite of the fact that society as a whole is getting increasingly dependent on it. When man came into being in the process of evolution, he was completely dependent on the natural environment. But slowly, over millions of years, this dependence of every individual person decreased: man learned how to make clothing from domesticated animals to protect himself from cold and to cultivate plants that provided him with food, and so forth. The most extreme degree of this independence is illustrated by modern megalopolises where man can live his whole life without ever once hearing the rustle of leaves, without bathing in a clean river or seeing a starry sky overhead. But at the same time the dependence of society as a whole on nature has grown sharply: on how much CO_2 and ozone there is in the atmosphere, on the presence of clean water, and keeping ecosystems in working order.

With all the said problems in mind, I would formulate the principal thesis of the new morality as follows: "We cannot command nature except by obeying her." This idea was first expressed by the great philosopher Francis Bacon back in 1620.

At the dawn of its life humanity had the so-called "paleolithic morality," the morality of the Stone Age, the main idea of which was the struggle against nature. That was followed by the "neolithic" morality, or the morality of the new Stone Age whose ideology was that of the conquest of nature. We live in the time of the morality of the scientific and technological revolution whose underlying motive is to make the fullest possible use of any natural resources within reach of the technologies available at any particular time.

All these moralities—paleolithic, neolithic, and technological—are the moralities of struggle and conquest. It is necessary to espouse the morality of protection and maintenance of nature, to adjust technologies to biospheric processes, to restore the environment that man has disrupted. This in my view is the content of the new morality or ecosophy.

RE   I share your feelings that we have reached the limit and that we cannot go on like this any longer.

Both of us agree that technology alone cannot resolve our problems and that our faith in its possibilities must not be so implicit. Homo sapiens must understand that knowledge, comprehension of facts, and their correct interpretation are at the basis of renewal. But this, too, is not enough to save the world.

We spoke on several occasions about the need for the new thinking, a concept that arises out of the interdependence of all things on this tiny speck in the universe. However, I don't go along with the assessments you cited of different forms of life. All that you mentioned cannot be judged in terms of money. The value of a species should be determined by its role in a broad interrelationship. If one such species drops out, this loss cannot be judged in dollars.

Although I understand the meaning of Bacon's aphorism, my sensibilities reject the very concept of "commanding nature," which hallows man's technological "attack" on his environment; I also do not accept Bacon's delimitation between man and nature because man is part of nature, like, say, a worm or a mollusk, a pine tree and a waterfall.

The new morality must imply that in their feelings and actions people will proceed from the close interrelationship between all the countless things that constitute our existence. But at the new level of our existence, equipped with fresh knowledge, we would regard this as a reversion to the days when the preindustrial man comprehended the world around him in his own way, and when he had not yet developed the arrogant attitude to the natural environment that, as you say, took the form of struggle against nature in order to conquer it.

In other words we have to restore the erstwhile contact with the fundamental principles of nature. Bacon must have meant exactly that, although he formulated this idea somewhat awkwardly.

You are right, saying that today the direct dependence of the individual on nature is as a whole not as strong as it was in the days of the preindustrial man. And yet in a sense this lesser dependence is imaginary. We have lived in close contact with nature for a long time and have grown with it; and every time we try to get away from it, we suffer from neuroses and feel somehow alienated in our own midst. There is even more concrete dependence. You must have indirectly come to this when you said that society has become even more dependent on nature. This has its imprint on all members of society, all individuals.

In this connection I have some ideas that have a direct bearing on what we said about ecomorality. It is hard to rely on the morality of the individual. It is much too easy to dampen the feelings of responsibility and mute the voice of "ecoconscience," saying that you are acting the way others act, or that all decisions to this effect are made by those at the top. To my mind the way to the responsibility of the individual lies through team morality. Technological globalism, the various decision-making procedures that often urge us toward short-term gain, production of goods geared to the consumer appetites of the day must all be countered by a team morality that presupposes a general responsibility and can in this way affect the personal position of every individual.

It goes without saying that, just like in many other cases, everything comes from interaction between a multitude of factors. Team morality does not get born, like Athena out of Zeus' head. It can only be the result of deep underlying processes, the combined efforts and will of a great multitude of individuals. New trends always take shape in the brains of individuals.

Sören A. Kierkegaard warned against a morality which can only blame, as if it were some sort of law. Such ethics, he said, cannot become effective because a ban is always countered by a desire for freedom and a search for loopholes. Today, as we fight for nature conservation, we resort to impositions of bans much too readily. Banning is unavoidable, but you really do not expect to go too far here. What we need is norms of behavior based on ecomorality, or ecosophy, which would integrate the growing amount of knowledge at our disposal.

Fear may, very possibly, come to our aid, a fear born of personal interests, of a desire to survive. I often watch fear, especially fear in young people. I think that they will yet have to drink that cup from the wells of fear. But fear may also be constructive if it shows us the dangers waylaying us, if it helps us concentrate on possibilities for warding them off. Fear may become one of the forces that creates a team ecological morality.

The very idea that to assume moral responsibility for the future is a difficult job may, paradoxically, help the individual to fight helplessness and encourage him to reject once and for all everything that might threaten the foundations of life.

A Y It looks as if there are two categories of people. Those of the first category feel that they are responsible for nature, and those of the other category who do not feel this responsibility. And here we revert to our old question: Has man separated himself from nature or is he still part of nature? Is man a social or biosocial being?

Therefore now and in the future the morality of these two categories of people will somewhat differ one from the other, although, in any event, this will be a new morality different from a current one. The technocrats will understand that nature protection underpins the stable development of humanity, that we cannot act upon nature with impunity and do anything we please with it just because technically we are equipped for it.

The protective shield of the atmosphere is getting weaker, the greenhouse effect is getting increasingly noticeable, the level of contamination of the global environment with different substances is such that man's behavior has, in some ways, changed, too; genetic deviations are putting ever greater pressure upon the human race. As a result, more and more abnormal children are born.

We have come to a dangerously high level of saturation of the biosphere with electromagnetic, noise, and light pollution. What is more, we have failed to retain the natural fertility of the soil. This explains why today people die from different causes from those in the past. A hundred years ago most deaths occurred from infectious and parasitic diseases, whereas today the principal causes of death in the industrial countries are cancer and coronary disorders. The environment created by industrial society is slowly killing its creator.

The same can be said about this problem, and indeed about the whole situation, when these are viewed through the prism of risk factors. The risk of being killed by lightning is negligible: one case per two million people a year. Actually, none of us takes such risk into account, as if it did not exist at all. The risk of dying of a snake bite in India is one case per five hundred thousand people. The risk of losing one's life in an air crash is much higher: one per one hundred thousand air passengers. But the risk of dying in an industrial accident is one per thirty thousand people. The risk of death in a road accident is one per five to ten thousand people. Now, getting closer to home, the risk of death from acid rain in the industrial countries is one per five thousand people; the risk of death from pesticide poisoning in high intensity farming areas is higher than one case per one thousand people. In many spheres of its activity humankind has approached the limit of admissible and acceptable risk. Moreover, the death rate connected with the anthropogenic impact on the environment has come up to and has, in some cases, exceeded the level of risk acceptable to society as a whole. I think that if we had the full statistics of disease and death on a region-to-region basis we would have a clearer picture of the critical state of the environment.

The mounting ecological threat—the fear of which you have mentioned—will compel even the most rigid technocrats to adopt ecomorality, which is not the whim of those who feel responsible for the natural environment. Ecomorality is the product of the unacceptability of the current technocratic trend in social development for the society of the future.

RE You have reminded me that some people feel very guilty for the way we have been treating the natural environment. You have con-

trasted these people to technocrats whose activities are dangerous to
the entire human race. Almost every day we come across representatives of these two opposing camps.

Nevertheless, the feeling of guilt, the feeling that you have committed an act of betrayal is typical of a greater number of people
than we generally think. It is just because this feeling is often
pinched out of our consciousness or at best takes the form of gnaw-
ing anxiety.

Of course, there are cynics who, without a trace of compunction,
encroach upon the fundamental conditions of life. It is against them
that we turn in anger. We do not want to follow blindly in their
footsteps.

I want to believe that the generation that has witnessed threats
to life mounting to catastrophic dimensions can direct its new intellectual and spiritual powers against these threats. Our expeditions in outer space must help us take a fresh look at our home in
the cosmos. Man has seen the planet Earth from outside, as it were.
And this has enabled him to understand how small is the stage on
which our human drama is being played out. Our Earth is so different from its other neighbors in the Solar System, with their craters
and glaciers. Spinning around the Sun, in the boundless black void
is a blue sphere with green, russet and red spots, the only haven of
life that we know exists in this part of the universe. Everything that
to us, citizens of the Earth, comes as something huge, is dwarfed:
the mountains look flattened out, the seas shallow. And the stone
frame of the planet is covered with an ever thinner film of soil that
is expected to feed everything living on Earth.

All these cosmic transformations dwarf our own fancied exclusive
position on this planet. We see ourselves as a sum total of the fragile
organization of life. Viewed from outside all our human contradictions—between individuals, groups and alliances —must be negligible, even meaningless.

It seems that to the generation that has grown up in the age of
fear this view from outside must stimulate a new thinking and a
new perception of the world, something you and I try to find. This
view from outside must also enable us to feel, comprehend with all

the fibers of our being that the Earth does not belong to all of us, but we all belong to the Earth.

This process is probably under way. We can see its tender shoots through the peace and green movements. These movements contain important impulses.

A Y You have given such a colorful view of the Earth from outer space. On my part I want to tell you about the cosmos that all of us carry with us wherever we go, and which we know so little about.

We are used to thinking that each one of us exists by himself. But now we can see that this is all wrong. Each one of us is a giant, a complex conglomerate of living beings. It exists in our intestines, in our lungs, and in other organs, with their billions of microscopic organisms. And it is only because these tiny organisms live inside us that we can digest the food we eat. The billions of wholesome bacteria on our skin cover us against pathogenic bacteria. We are not ill because these friends of ours live on the surface of our skin. Our entire health and our physical well-being depend on the well-being and on the well-coordinated action of the microcosm that each one of us has.

We are only now starting really to understand this microcosm, and it is only now that we are beginning to understand ourselves. But even now it is getting increasingly clear that the physico-chemical surroundings we have created in our industrial era bode nothing good for this microcosm.

I shall attempt to outline some principles of ecomorality the way in which not only I but indeed many other scientists visualize them.

First. When it separated out from nature the human race learned how to direct the development of nature. However, the scope of such directing will always be rather limited because man will always remain part of nature. Therefore the protection of nature and its thrifty, nonexpendable utilization is the indispensable condition for the successful development of the human race.

Second. Destroyed species cannot be restored. The loss of the genetic variety of animate nature has left a gap that will never be healed. This disappearance of species is much more dangerous than the depletion of energy sources or any political problems. Of all the ecological hazards the loss of genetic variety is the greatest danger for humanity.

Third. Population growth and a simultaneous rise in the well-being of society are impossible, considering the limited resources of the ecosystems of our planet.

Fourth, and finally. The importance of the preservation of the biosphere must be given priority in any system of values, and in decision making. The preservation of the ecosystems and the biosphere as a whole is most important for humanity, considering the need for its further development on the planet.

As I cite these principles I do not pretend to an all-embracing description of ecomorality. Yet I think that they must be consonant with any ecomorality, whatever its wording, no matter who tries to formulate it.

RE The above four principles can well sum up what we have been talking about all these days. This is the quintessence of what should be the practical application of ecosophy.

I'm again turning to this concept. The words ecology and ecosophy come from the Greek word *oikos*, or house. Thus ecology is a science about our home, and about our little house in the Universe. We need this knowledge in order to keep this house in order. The term "ecosophy" can be translated as "the wise judgment about the house," which suggests a concept based on ecological knowledge. Ecosophy has not gained currency so far. Now we need it more than we have at any other time.

You were quite right when you spoke about the cosmos within us. Just as you, I believe that we not only discover our Earth from outside, but actually look at the cosmos within us with the help of astrophysics and physics of elementary particles. This new perspective links us with other living organisms.

And on this speck of cosmic dust called the Earth, we are destined to be a species with the help of which the cosmos—which is so infinitely large and at the same time so infinitely small—can look at itself, can meditate over its own essence. The awareness of this must make us more and more responsible for life in our cosmic house. We, just as anyone on the planet, are a product of the Earth's evolution, but in view of our consciousness and our ability to think, we are responsible for its further evolution. This is the responsibility no other living creature has ever borne. As a species we must learn how to contain ourselves in order to direct further development.

When we look at our Earth from outside, as one integral whole, we cannot help feeling that no individual, no company, no country, and no generation of people are entitled to master anything, in the direct sense of the word, be it soil, water, or air. This feeling must underlie our profound understanding that we have been trusted to be the guardians of the great wealth that has been in existence over tremendous periods of time and which we, after our quick sojourn on the Earth, must hand over to future generations.

A Y You are talking like a Marxist.

R E You may call me anything you want. I am championing what you might call ecological socialism. I call it guardianship.

Before we move any further, let's sort out the various definitions we have been using. This will do us some good, no doubt. For me the ideal society is a democratic system that would enable individual citizens as much as possible to steer decision making to the point where it has a direct effect on their life. Of course, the Western style of democracy has a lot of drawbacks. And yet, to my mind, it provides the individual with a lot more degrees of freedom than a rigidly centralized system.

However, no society in the world is a closed system, for it develops in one direction or another. Quite possibly, the Western democracies will develop toward greater centralization in some sectors in order to restrain some of the more stridently unbridled forces of the market, whereas the countries with rigid centralization will eventually let up on this rigidity. As far as I understand, herein lies one of the objectives of perestroika in your country. In other words, as we noted on the first day of our dialogue, the stubborn contention that capitalism and communism are incompatible is more stereotypic than realistic. I would like to add here that with all the obvious factual differences between these formations, both of them are full of problems and neither of them will ever be able to survive an ecological collapse or a nuclear war. As John Galbraith said, nobody will ever be able to tell capitalist ashes from communist ashes.

In other words, we are bound together with common fears and threats, regardless of our ideologies. Hence the simple conclusion: having recognized the existence of different political doctrines and systems, we must cooperate with each other in order to solve the problems of survival which are common to all of us.

A Y This is what we in the USSR now call the new political thinking. Regrettably, many people have not fully understood this.

R E I would introduce into the new thinking, which both of us regard as necessary, a meaning which possibly no country, regardless of its political system and ideology, is prepared to accept. To my mind, in order to solve the problem of survival, we need some form of world administration vested with the finite responsibility for governing planetary resources. This means that certain countries, whether big or small, or even super-large, would have to be prepared to surrender much of their sovereignty.

A Y I am afraid this might lead to some sort of global centralism that you are so reluctant to see in individual countries.

R E I am quite aware of the risk of global technocracy, which one anti-utopian has called ecofascism. To my mind this model should be an international administration that will keep an eye on the resources of the Earth and that will determine their limits and work out an ecological budget according to which the expenditure of natural resources must not exceed the reproductive capacities of nature. At the same time measures should be taken to steer clear of gigantism that increases the distance between those who make decisions and those who are on the recipient end of these decisions. In its concrete forms, administration of local resources could be conducted by smaller communities. Thus it would be possible to decentralize globalism and put responsibility back into the hands of those who had to give up their formal sovereignty. The ultimate variant is to entrust practical actions to agricultural associations and other small groups whose participation would make people feel that what is being done has a direct bearing on the environment in which they live.

I agree that this is an ideal model. In practical terms it is extremely difficult to cause the state to abandon their formal sovereignty or to coordinate the actions of the central government, on the one hand, and regional areas of responsibility, on the other.

Of course, it is always easier to envision our future than to try and alter something that actually exists. Yet I trust we can turn these images of the future into a reality.

A Y   On the one hand, I want to argue with you. And on the other, I feel that political differences must be relegated to the background in the face of the global problems facing humankind today. I shall repeat again that this, in substance, is the new political thinking that the whole world is talking about.

But let's agree on the terminology we are going to use. I think it would be more appropriate to speak about socialization of nature rather than about ecological socialism. There are so many "socialisms" in the modern world—democratic, real and other. We would get all mixed up in different "socialisms." But what we are talking about is socialization of nature. Of course, this is just terminology, but it is very important for the proper understanding of the subject of our discussion.

All the more so since there are books on the subject, such as one called *Socialization de la nature* by the Frenchman Philippe Saint-Marc.

R E   I have no objections to your terminological specifications. Of course one cannot put a sign of equality between socialization of nature and socialist ideology.

There is one thing I would like to add. Since all citizens of the Earth, during their brief sojourn here, bear collective responsibility for their planet and its future, society must allow for freedom of the individual so that each can pass from one room to another in this large, common house. It is not fair that today we have opened the doors just a little for people who want to part with conditions they find unbearable. Still worse, in my view, is the situation when people are not allowed to leave the country where they were by fate born. On a small celestial body where all people are dependent on one another, people must be allowed to move around, encountering no obstacles, be it walls or barbed wire.

Actually, all new thoughts, ideas, and innovations should be held in common ownership by all humankind. The attempts being made today to prevent the achievements of science and technology in one country from being the property of other countries are motivated by a social philosophy that we should have long since abandoned. We even saw some enterprising people claiming the property rights to the knowledge of human genes. Recently, one scientist, a Nobel prize winner, wished to take out a patent for the results of his research into certain parts of the human hereditary factor. He claimed that there was no difference between a work of literature safeguarded by copyright and cyclic nucleotides in some part of a gene, that in both cases the problem in question was a mere combination of letters, except that in the second case, the combination of letters was from the genetic alphabet. This is a curious example of how people working in such advanced fields are still captives of the old thinking. The achievements of the inquisitive human mind must belong to the whole of human society.

A Y Maybe the Royal Academy of Sciences of Sweden, which awarded the Nobel prize to this scientist, should not have done so? To be serious, it is hard to answer all the questions you have raised. It seems to me that some of them need not be answered: you just voiced your point of view that deserves to be treated with respect.

I also think that in our common house here on Earth we must all have common rules of behavior. And, of course, the doors in this house must stay open. But just imagine this situation. Somebody decided to enter the room of a young couple on their wedding night. Do you think this would be an appropriate thing to do? Or somebody starts up a family squabble. Or a very ill person in this house should be left undisturbed. Sharing your idea that the doors of our house should stay open for all, I am positive that we should observe the rules of propriety. As for your idea that any person should be allowed to resettle, I think it's quite correct, and I don't think I should conceal my views on this subject, although I don't think everybody in my country shares them. Just like other countries, the Soviet Union must allow free exit to all those who wish to leave it and, conversely, must allow free access to all people except criminals, fugitives from justice.

I would like to enlarge upon the idea of socialization of nature. Irrespective of our desire, this process is under way in different countries.

The fact that the process of socialization is sometimes manifest in capitalist countries seems to me quite indicative. I was pleased to know that in Sweden every person has the right to visit and spend a night in any forest, no matter who its owner may be. You say that this is an old custom. All I can say is that this custom reflects very well the inalienable right of every person to the bounties of nature. Several years ago a law was passed in Italy under which the people of the country are entitled to the public use of the seashore. Thus each Italian has the right to the beach. Similar legal norms have been introduced in some states in the United States for the use of riverbanks. In France, where two-thirds of all forest land is privately owned, the law binds forest owners to carry out the necessary forest protection measures (on penalty of expropriation of the forest). Some forests in France can be declared protected areas in public interests, regardless of who they may belong to. Even in Britain a law was recently passed prohibiting the owners to change the landscape at will. This, I think, is an element of socialization of nature.

In addition to socialization from "above," there is a counter-process, socialization "from below." This takes the form of a public movement for the purchase of land by different public organizations for setting up new national parks and other protected zones. In many countries, notably in the United States and Britain, whenever people want to save their territory from depredation they raise funds for buying this territory and put it under public protection. What is it, then, but socialization of nature.

So as you see, socialization of nature is taking place in different countries: in Sweden with its old bourgeois-democratic traditions, in Italy and Britain, and, of course, in my country and other socialist countries where nature is, constitutionally, public property. It looks as if everywhere people are beginning to use their right to share in the benefits of nature, a right that has been forgotten in some places. I think that this process will continue to develop in the future. I feel quite optimistic about it.

RE You are referring to the Swedish right to the common use of land. As you have said, this is an old, traditional, and unique right characteristic of our part of the world. You can freely wander about the forest, gathering mushrooms and berries, or set up a tent in picturesque places. All you are required to do is to be careful. The right to public use of the forest is not restricted by the legal forms of ownership. Forests may belong to the state, to private citizens, and companies. The state is entitled to intervene with the way private citizens and companies look after the forest; it also has the right to declare a forest a restricted zone on certain sections of coast and also to prohibit the use of projects that might change the normal course of waterflow in rivers. The Swedish parliament has endorsed a master plan for utilization of both waters and forests. All that can well be interpreted as socialist threads in the fabric of a mixed economy. I am convinced that the number of such threads should be increased.

The examples you have given—and I can give you many more of them—show that in many parts of the world efforts are being made to expand such constructive practices, although the institution of global administration is still far away.

Our exchange of views has over the past several days led me to still another thought. We must not shut our eyes to the fact that scientists are often compelled to do things that may lead to the suicide of the human race. This concerns research in the military field and in civic production that is fraught with baneful consequences for the environment.

A long time ago Galileo Galilei came down upon clergymen who wanted to subject science to their influence. Eventually, science freed itself from the influence of the church. Nevertheless, the drama is continuing in our days, because the church dogmas are often replaced by those of the state. In our time, too, we have our own heretics, our own Galileis both in the West and in the East. Nevertheless, we cannot say that science is fully free.

It often happens that large companies and capitalist firms restrict the right of the scientist to pursue his independent course. Many scientists behaved very obsequiously when they were offered lucrative jobs on projects dangerous to their fellow citizens. A good example of this is the SDI, which we have already spoken about.

I am asking myself if the time has not come for scientists, especially those who do research in natural sciences, to take something similar to the Hippocratic oath, a pledge not to take part in research that is harmful to the human race. What would you say to that, Alexei?

A Y A very good idea. I think we could make this proposal to all scientists: every engineer and every scientist must take such an oath. One of its provisions says: "Do no harm!" And this is exactly what nature needs so much now. So I think that this is an excellent suggestion, and I support it wholeheartedly.

We have discussed many things. It looks as if we have discussed all our questions. All except one. We spoke about socialization of nature as carried out within national boundaries. However, there is still another process taking place alongside this socialization. What I have in mind is internationalization of nature. To save the natural environment of our planet, and indeed to save themselves, some countries forfeit some of their national sovereignty and liberty. This is not ecofascism, but real life. We know that there are many international agreements (their number growing) under which some nations voluntarily undertake to regiment or limit their activities. At one of our early meetings we spoke about Club–30, an international agreement on limiting the discharge of sulfur and on transborder transportation of acid rain. There are many conventions on the protection and utilization of natural resources in some regions (Antarctic, South America, Western Europe, etc.), that impose definite obligations upon the signatory states to refrain from certain activities. I think the number of such voluntarily assumed obligations for the protection of nature will grow still further.

One does not have to have a vivid imagination to see that in the not too distant future certain international bodies will be set up to work out "a code of ecological behavior" for the countries of Europe or other parts of the world—Central and Southern Asia, the Americas, Africa. It is hard to tell now what form such obligations will take.

Can existing bodies do that? It looks as if the specialized agencies of the United Nations are not yet ready to become such ecologico-political centers. A great deal of work in this direction is being done by the European Parliament where only the countries of the West are represented. But the idea is to coordinate in the best possible way the ecological policy of all countries in every geographical region.

The first step in this direction has become the creation of national ecological strategies. This idea was initiated several years ago by the International Union for Conservation of Nature and Natural Resources. Today more than forty countries have created their national strategies of nature conservation. Actually, these are ecological strategies. The second step should be coordination and then unification of the national ecological strategies of closely situated countries. This would inevitably lead to the creation of ecological centers for providing recommendations on the development of large natural zones. One such recommendation is the creation of a pan-European ecoparliament. I think all this is not so fantastic as it seems. The Helsinki accords signalled the first step in this direction, when countries with different political systems decided that it was necessary to unify their legislation on nature conservation. Regrettably, work in this direction has slowed down, possibly because the public does not prod politicians in this direction persistently enough.

I would be glad if our dialogue served to enliven this movement. Why not daydream a little about a global ecological government? Incidentally, futurologists have long since been talking about a world government, meaning global administration of society. Very possibly, long before the creation of a world government, which is still a matter of a distant future, something of a world ecoparliament will be set up.

Of course, we must keep in close touch with national traditions and avoid any hint at ecofascism, which you spoke about early on. Nevertheless, states must ever more closely coordinate their ecological policy as soon as possible. This can hardly be achieved without a special agency.

Global ecological management will not hurt either freedom of the individual, or the sovereignty of individual countries. After all, freedom is realized necessity. If we realize fully that we must not discharge toxic substances into the air or water, that pesticides must not be used uncontrollably, then we can ban such practices. These would be restrictions that sovereign nations would accept conscientiously in order to save life on Earth and to assure the continuance of the human race. Isn't that so?

RE I think, too, that a world regime of environmental management cannot be introduced by a single decision. No matter how necessary it would be, this regime could, to my mind, be achieved only through stage-by-stage agreements.

We can have conventions or any other accords for different areas of human activity. You mentioned Club–30, a group of countries that have agreed to enforce a 30 percent reduction in sulfur discharge by 1993. In the same vein, about forty countries have pledged to slowly reduce the discharge of fluorides so that by the end of this century this discharge will be reduced by half. The problem is that in both cases the level of such reductions is much too small.

As for the freon, Sweden has gone much farther than any other country by undertaking to reduce their discharge by half by 1990, and then to stop their production altogether in four years. In addition to that we are planning to set up an international institute for the technical aspects of environmental problems. We have a special envoy who keeps in touch with other countries over environmental protection.

To achieve this objective in stages, it would also be expedient to draw up regional accords. Such an accord already exists among the northern countries. Another region of cooperation is the Baltic countries that are greatly concerned about the marine environment, a project in which you participate. The countries of the North Sea also have their own convention. They seem to be tackling ecological problems in earnest. Europe, with its many smaller states, which contaminate one another with toxin-laden wind and water, is badly in need of transborder cooperation in order to put an end to this outrage. The network of such regional accords may serve as a forerunner of a global system.

I do not think that the creation of a world political government is possible, not in the near future anyway. However, we can already visualize the institution of specialized administrations or so-called "target-oriented federations." A few years ago I expressed an idea about setting up an oceanic administration to regulate the regime of the ocean that belongs to all people. I also suggested the setting up of an energy administration to control the use of energy resources of our planet and to encourage the search for new sources of energy. In the sphere of ecology I think it possible to set up a global administration to tackle the tasks we have been discussing. I do not know how all these problems can be dealt with from the political point of view. What I am quite sure of is that this process must proceed in stages, which, of course, raises the problem of how soon all this can be achieved.

A Y   This process is already under way. There is not a single major political party in any country that does not include ecological demands in its program. In ten or twenty years from now such political programs may well turn into ecological manifestos. And that is only a few steps away from a world ecological administration.

RE I sincerely hope you are right!

AY The joint and coordinated management of air, water, and ocean resources must serve as some sort of powerful "institute of international accord" that would stabilize the present shaky political world. I do not exclude the possibility that the ecological imperative may soon become a political imperative. We say: "Every cloud has a silver lining." So it could well be that the catastrophic state of the biosphere will serve as a powerful impetus for strengthening world peace.

RE Looking back one can see that our whole history has been influenced by man's attitude to the environment. And our future depends on how we shall interact with our environment.

Once Franz Kafka thought up a bitter aphorism: "There is an infinite hope, but not for us." I don't believe in this "infinite hope," either, but I firmly believe that there is hope, just hope. Our mind has a distinctive bent for self-destruction. At the same time it has vast potential for development. I trust in man's desire to keep the spark of life burning, the spark that will help him to overcome the crisis he himself has precipitated.

I believe in man's future, not necessarily a future that is so much better, but a future that is tolerably good. I draw this belief from my observations of the young generation. I myself belong to the generation that saw new horizons, saw the changing picture of the world, to the generation which has interpreted the unity of the universe in a new way, but which has failed to get rid of the ossified behavioral patterns and to break up the routine of life. The present young generation is free from the burden of routine, the burden of standard behavior. It is not inhibited by the mistakes and oversights of my generation.

Many young people are free from dogmatism and therefore treat their seniors with a grain of skepticism. Therein lies their strength, and therein lies our hope: "If the children of the Stone Age followed in the footsteps of their parents, we would still be living in the Stone Age."

I do not particularly relish rock music. But there must be something attractive about it to the youth throughout the world. Very possibly, this is one of the ways the youth protest against commercialization in the West, against bureaucratization in the East, against everything that has muddled up the life of the older generation. The young generation has something that unites them across all borders. I think at times that the young people of the West and East have more in common than they have with the older generation in their own country. And if young people in different countries eventually wake up to the awareness that solidarity between them is strong, they will force those at the helm to make the ship of state change its course.

As I listen to the voices of some young people I feel more and more strongly that our present age—with its world wars, with its maniacal armaments drive, its tribulations and destruction, and its depredation of the environment—will come to the next generation as one of the most dismal chapters in the history of the human race.

Vladimir Vysotsky, your famous bard, in his "Song of the Earth" expressed something that concerns the young people of all the continents:

> Ugly trenches have cut the terrain,
> And deep craters like wounds are spread open,
> Naked nerves of the Earth are in pain,
> Their sufferings are more than awful,
> It will stand, it will last, it will live,
> Don't regard our Earth as a cripple,
> Who has said that the Earth sings no more,
> And provides no joy to its people?!
> No, it rings, muffling moans and whines,
> With its wounds, with its scars, with its craters.
> After all, our Earth is our soil,
> That surrenders to no violators!

There is an image that often sets me to thinking. On the North Pole all meridians converge at one point. There is neither East nor West there. And only there, away from that point, where the meridians begin to diverge, do countries and peoples drift apart and then turn against one another.

And since the Earth is round, one can say that cosmic forces have created it so that we could meet. Over the past several decades the new means of communication and the possibility of looking at the Earth from outer space have made our planet so small that the meridians of all our mistakes must converge at one point, the point of understanding and cooperation.

Rudyard Kipling's words "Oh, East is East, and West is West, and never the twain shall meet" sound in today's world as some sort of echo from long gone days.

A Y Before we finish our dialogue I would like to say a few more words. At the beginning we were beset by our common troubles and concerns about the future of the Earth. As we went on we exchanged our views and our thoughts about what we now think are many important, indeed, very important problems of nature protection and about the development of the human race on Earth. We even argued over some questions. But, to my surprise, our points of view either concurred or were very close to one another on most issues. And this gives me the idea that to the reader our dialogue may sound very much like a duet.

Both of us agree that time is running out for the solution of ecological problems. The Soviet author Valentin Rasputin, in one of his public appearances, read out a letter he had received from a Soviet industrial worker. That man had been near the Chernobyl nuclear power station at the time of the accident. This is what he wrote to Rasputin: "I agree to live even in a cave by the light of a burning wick. All I want is life."

Healthy life will be an increasingly difficult problem for more and more people if the present technocratic trends in society prevail.

The American philosopher Henry D. Thoreau said more than a hundred years ago: "Morning is when I am awake and there is a dawn in me." Our dialogue is just another attempt to awaken the sleeping ones.

You spoke so well about the hopes we place on the young generation. We must not conceal our doubts from them, and I hope that our dialogue will be helpful. We have tried to set the record straight without mincing words. The young people will still have to solve many problems created by the older generations.

This dialogue, I hope, will attract the attention of politicians, industrialists, and other leaders who make decisions but who, at the same time, often forget about ecology, about their responsibility for tomorrow.

Sometimes they do not even visualize the future of their own countries, just because they cannot see past their immediate political and economic concerns. Civilization on Earth can be preserved provided two conditions are observed: peace on Earth, and harmony between the human race and nature. This is something nobody should ever forget.

RE You are quite right. After the seven days we have spent together we have found out that there are a lot more things that bring us closer together than things that keep us apart. We have met as two concerned citizens among five billion others. Very possibly our dialogue is valuable in that our views have coincided on so many issues. I think that if the number of such dialogues across ideological frontiers increased, people would to their great surprise see how much there is in this world that brings them closer together.

Speaking of what man should do in order to cope with the nuclear and ecological threats he has himself created, we concluded that he is running a race against time. In the biblical story about the creation of the world, God, within six days, created water, the soil, plants, animals, and, finally, He created man on the deserted and lonely Earth. And when, on the seventh day, He took a rest from his labors He said: "This is good!"

Everything in nature is cause and effect. At some stage of evolution one active cause was man. He became a geological force that transforms the surface of the Earth, that changes forests, water, air, all those things without which life would be impossible. Consumed by our pride and conceit we thought for a long time that by so doing we would improve the conditions of our life. Now we know that none of us can say about our doings: "This is good!"

We have applied our creative efforts at the wrong end and in the wrong direction, threatening to turn the Earth back into a lonely and deserted place. To make sure that life will continue, we must stop the process we ourselves initiated and do so now. Tomorrow will be too late!

INDEX